nüFEKOP

**IMAGES
OF A CLASSIC
GAME COMPANY**

By Scott Elder

© 2010 By Scott Elder All Rights Reserved. All Photos and digital captures are property of the author.

Except as permitted under the United States Copyright Act of 1976, no part of this publication may be reproduced or distributed in any form or by any means without the prior written permission of the publisher.

Printing (01) 02 03 04 05 06 07 08 09

The names "Commodore", "Vic 20", "C-64" are © and TM Commodore Business Machines and are owned by Commodore International Corporation. The author is in no way affiliated with C.I.C.

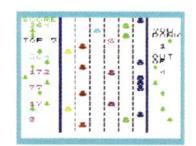

Introduction.

I wish to document what I have remaining, in my head and in physical property, about this small but influential software company.

Nüfekop wrote and published game titles for the Vic 20 and Commodore 64 computers. This was in the early 80's when home computing was finally coming of age. Personal gaming systems like the Atari 2600 and Magnavox Odyssey were finding their way into homes, but computers were not widely sold for home use. They were very expensive and thus limited to serious enthusiasts. Commodore would soon change all that. When they introduced the Vic 20 in 1981 at around $300.00, it allowed a much wider audience to get involved in home computing.

Arcades were also peaking at that time and nearly everyone was playing videogames. The natural evolution of that was to have the games at home. At first, that task was left to several small companies, as the larger companies took a couple years to get game software distribution figured out. Nüfekop was the poster child for starting a business in a bedroom, moving it to a garage, then renting an office, and finally buying property and building a warehouse.

My name is Scott Elder, co-founder of Nüfekop. The following pages contain material I've managed to save from back in the day, I hope you enjoy looking at them. I feel better knowing that this creativity is preserved in this book you now have in your hands.

Enjoy!

What's in a name?

We were really struggling coming up with a name, knowing we were doing games, we wanted to stress "FUN". Looking for inspiration we also ran through much of the basic programming language and liked the word "Poke", which was used to set a byte of memory. Co-founder Gary Elder put them together and reversed them, later coming up with a "Druid" backstory about Nüfekop and stonehenge.

The name was fun to play with and people remembered it.

In a Compute! Magazine letter to the editor, this ran:
In your review of the latest games from Nüfekop Software (February 1983, p. 140), you write: "the word Nüfekop, according to the firm's early ads, has a Druid origin, and means putting an extraordinarily large amount into a small pocket or enclosure, possibly through the use of magic."

This must have been tongue-in-cheek. Surely you recognize "poke fun" spelled backwards.

Gary Elder of Nüfekop, responds:

We were completely shocked, but it's true! We're amazed, as always, at the visionary powers of the Druids.

Here is some early Nüfekop letterhead.

If you got a letter from us, it was probably in an envelope like this.

Scott Who?

I was eighteen when Nüfekop formed. If I had to describe myself I would say I was a decent mechanic that loved to race motocross. I was a "C" student in high school simply because I couldn't stand being cooped up in a classroom. Didn't have much interest in anything else but motorcycles.
My brother Gary had purchased a used computer, an Ohio Scientific 2P.
It had an early basic and I'm pretty sure it was 6502 based. I played a few very crude games on it, most were turn based adventure games, hardly any graphics. My brothers and I tinkered with that machine for hours learning to program.
What was a surprise to me is that I had a bit of natural talent for writing code. It just made sense to me. I didn't get tangled up in complexity like I witnessed so many others doing. I think my simpler take on things helped, as I wasn't nearly as accomplished in math as my siblings, yet I could program without much effort.
What happened next was the Vic 20 was released. It was very fun with it's color graphics and modifiable character set. I quickly wrote a few games and we were all playing them, not thinking about anything bigger than that.
A computer enthusiast friend was visiting and played some of the games. He was soon talking about the need to sell these, that they were marketable. Gary quickly started formulating plans, my brother Steve and I with help from younger brother Keith went to work making enough games to fill a catalog, and within weeks Nüfekop was underway.

Who am I, why the "brother of invention" of course (ha). Our state accident provider had some money to burn and ran this in newspapers around Oregon, and did a similar radio spot where Gary and I horribly read horrible dialog.

THE BROTHER OF INVENTION

Scott Elder's home in the southern Oregon town of Shady Cove seems an unlikely place for hyperspace battles.

But since he was 16, Scott has been writing innovative computer games there that have been a hit from Sweden to Sydney.

Now Scott and brother Gary mass produce the games under their "Nufekop" company brand, creating needed jobs in Shady Cove.

Inventiveness helped the Elder brothers capture a share of the computer game market. That's good for Oregon. And it's why we're proud they chose SAIF Corporation to provide their workers' compensation insurance.

SAIF CORPORATION

Our first Catalog.

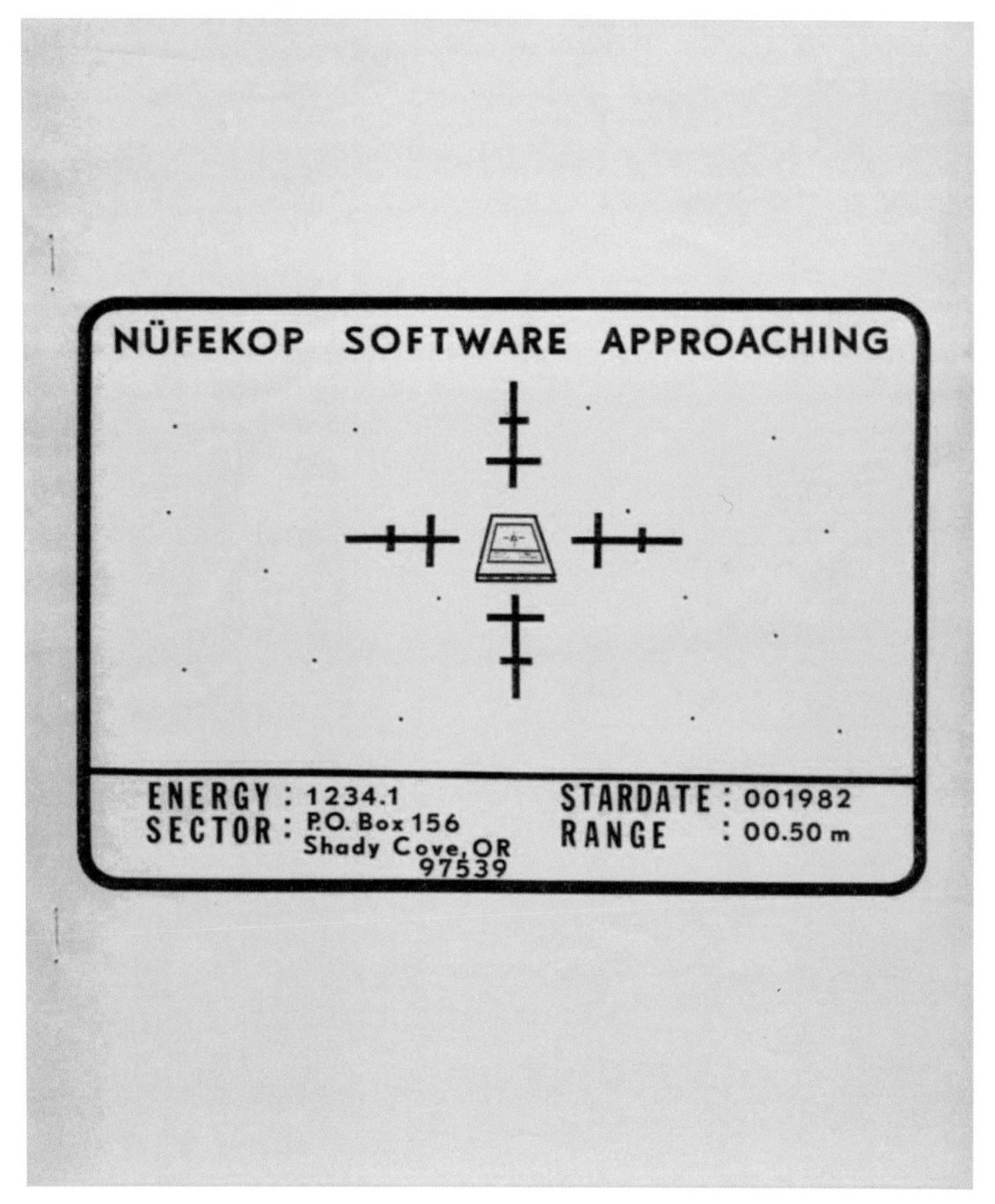

```
NÜFEKOP  SOFTWARE  APPROACHING
```

ENERGY : 1234.1   STARDATE : 001982
SECTOR : P.O. Box 156   RANGE   : 00.50 m
         Shady Cove, OR
             97539

This was done using pinstripe tape, transfer lettering and an antique typewriter. It couldn't have been much more amateurish, but it did convey an element of fun, so it worked out very well for us.

Introduction

FIRST OFF, WE'D LIKE TO THANK YOU FOR BEING INTERESTED IN OUR SOFTWARE, WE KNOW THAT YOU WON'T REGRET IT. ALL OUR GAMES ARE "PLAY TESTED", BY KIDS, GRANDADS, ARCADE WIZARDS, AND ANYONE THAT WE CAN PULL OFF THE STREET. WE WOULD ALSO LIKE TO SHARE OUR THOUGHTS ON COMPUTER GAMES AND REAL TIME. OUR PROGRAMS ARE WRITTEN SO THAT THEY ARE FUN TO PLAY. A LOT OF AUTHORS COULD WRITE SOME PRETTY GOOD PROGRAMS, BUT IF THEY'RE NOT FUN, THEY SHOULD NOT BE CALLED GAMES. ALSO, ALL OUR GAMES THAT SHOULD(ESPECIALLY ARCADE TYPE GAMES) DO RUN IN REAL TIME, WHICH MEANS THAT THE ACTION DOESN'T STOP JUST BECAUSE YOU FIRED A MISSILE, OR BECAUSE THE COMPUTER MADE IT'S MOVE, ETC., JUST LIKE IN THE ARCADES. SO PLAY HARD, BUT HAVE FUN!

ALL PROGRAMS IN THIS CATALOG (UNLESS OTHERWISE SPECIFIED) ARE ON CASSETTE TAPE, RECORDED ONCE ON EACH SIDE, AND WILL RUN ON ANY COMMODORE VIC 20 COMPUTER WITH 5K OF MEMORY. ALSO, MOST GAMES ARE AVAILABLE FOR USE WITH EITHER KEYBOARD OR JOYSTICK CONTROLS. THIS MEANS THE GAME IS AVAILABLE IN A VERSION THAT USES ATARI JOYSTICK CONTROLLERS. PLEASE SPECIFY KEYBOARD OR JOYSTICK IN SPACE PROVIDED ON ORDER BLANK. VERY IMPORTANT.

Games

INVASION
YOU ARE ON A MISSION TO PROTECT THE VERY VALUEABLE ENERGY PODS FROM THE INVADING ALIEN SHIPS. YOU CAN DROP BOMBS OR FIRE ROCKETS THAT MUST DESTROY THE ENEMY. VERY CHALLENGING GAME.
AVAILABLE IN KEYBOARD OR JOYSTICK VERSIONS.
CG036 ----- INVASION ----- $9.99

RACEWAY
HERE IS THE GAME FOR CAR RACE FANS. ONE OR TWO PLAYERS CAN RACE AGAINST TIME OR AGAINST EACH OTHER. FEATURES VERY FAST ACTION, CHOICE OF OVAL TRACK OR A VERY COMPLEX, TWISTY, CHALLENGING TRACK, AND A TIMER THAT DISPLAYS YOUR E.T. DOWN TO SIXTIETH'S OF SECONDS.
AVAILABLE IN KEYBOARD VERSION ONLY.
CG032 ----- RACEWAY ----- $9.99

KRAZY KONG
THE CRAZY GORILLA HAS TAKEN THREE FAIR MAIDENS UP TO THE TOP OF THE GIANT STAIRWAY AND YOU (BEING THE VALIANT HERO THAT YOU ARE) WILL ATTEMPT TO RESCUE THEM AT THE RISK OF YOUR OWN LIFE. YOUR TIMING MUST BE TOTALLY ACCURATE AS YOU JUMP THE BARRELS THAT KONG IS ROLLING DOWN AT YOU.
AVAILABLE IN KEYBOARD OR JOYSTICK VERSIONS.
CG054 ----- KRAZY KONG ----- $9.99

Do you remember buying games on cassette tape? At this point in time that's the only way you could buy them. A couple years later you could get them on 5 ¼ " floppies.

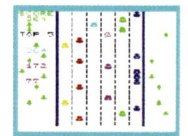

Arcade games were all the rage, so you had to sell knock-offs of the popular games, it's what everyone wanted. Vikman was obviously one of those. It was not a very good game, but it was one of first copies actually available on the Vic and sold really well.

VIKMAN

THIS WELL KNOWN GAME IS A FAVORITE OF COMPUTER GAMERS. SIMILIAR TO THE ARCADE GAME, YOU MUNCH YOUR WAY AROUND A MAZE EATING DOTS, AND AVOIDING THE MONSTERS (UNLESS YOU'VE EATEN A POWER DOT, THEN THEY'LL RUN). VIKMAN ALSO HAS AN OPTION WHERE YOU CHOOSE HOW MANY MONSTERS YOU WANT.
AVAILABLE IN KEYBOARD OR JOYSTICK VERSIONS.
CG002 ----- VIKMAN ----- $9.99

QUIRK

FOR YOU PEOPLE WHO CAN'T SIT STILL, WE HAVE A GAME THAT'LL KEEP YOU HOPPING. BY JUMPING THROUGH HOLES IN THE MOVING FLOORS YOU ATTEMPT TO CATCH FALLING OBJECTS BEFORE THEY HIT THE BOTTOM LEVEL. IF YOU CAN JUMP TO THE TOP FLOOR YOU CAN GET AN ENERGIZER POD THAT INCREASES THE POINTS OF THE PRIZES YOU CATCH. QUICK REACTIONS ARE A MUST IN THIS VERY ADDICTING GAME.
AVAILABLE IN KEYBOARD OR JOYSTICK VERSIONS.
CG044 ----- QUIRK ----- $9.99

TARGET

TARGET IS A FAST PACED GAME THAT REQUIRES QUICK THINKING AND EVEN QUICKER REACTIONS. AS YOU COLLECT POINTS BY RUNNING INTO THE TARGETS, YOUR SPEED INCREASES AND YOUR TAIL GETS LONGER INCREASING DIFFICULTY.
AVAILABLE IN KEYBOARD OR JOYSTICK VERSIONS.
CG016 ----- TARGET ----- $9.99

BOMBER

YOU ARE IN CHARGE OF THREE DIFFERENT AIRCRAFT ON A MISSION TO CLEAR OUT A CANYON. YOU MUST PICK YOUR TARGET CAREFULLY AND DROP YOUR BOMBS QUICKLY AND VERY ACCURATELY TO AVOID WASTING PRECIOUS TIME. EASY TO CATCH ON TO, BUT VERY HARD TO MASTER.
AVAILABLE IN KEYBOARD OR JOYSTICK VERSIONS.
CG014 ----- BOMBER ----- $9.99

RESCUE FROM NÜFON

HERE IS THE GAME THAT CONTAINS MORE THAN YOU (OR WE) THOUGHT POSSIBLE IN A STANDARD 5K VIC. RESCUE FROM NUFON IS AN ADVENTURE TYPE GAME THAT HAS OVER A HUNDRED ROOMS SPREAD OUT OVER FIVE FLOORS. YOUR MISSION IS TO BEAM DOWN TO AN ALIEN BUILDING AND TRANSPORT ALL THE HUMANS THAT YOU CAN LOCATE BACK UP TO THE MOTHER SHIP. YOU HAVE A LIMITED AMOUNT OF ENERGY, WHICH WILL LAST YOU FOR QUITE A LONG TIME, UNLESS YOU HAVE A RUN-IN WITH ONE OF THE FOUR SPECIES OF ALIENS OCCUPYING THE BUILDING. IT ACCEPTS ONE KEY COMMANDS, SOME OF WHICH ARE; NORTH, SOUTH, EAST, WEST, TRANSPORT, FIRE, UP, DOWN, ETC..
SO IF YOU ARE A PERSON WHO ENJOYS A CHALLENGING ADVENTURE, YET STILL WANTS GRAPHICS DISPLAYS OF WHAT THEY'RE PLAYING, NUFON IS THE PLACE FOR YOU.
AVAILABLE IN KEYBOARD VERSION ONLY.
CG058 ----- RESCUE FROM NUFON ----- $9.99

DODGECARS

IF YOU HAVE EVER WONDERED WHAT IT WOULD BE LIKE TO BE GOING THE WRONG WAY ON A FREEWAY THEN YOU REALLY OUGHT TO TRY THIS GAME. YOU MUST DODGE THE EVER-INCREASING TRAFFIC WITH THE HOPE THAT YOU CAN STAY ALIVE JUST A LITTLE LONGER. THE FAST, SMOOTH ACTION OF THIS GAME MAKES IT ONE OF THE MOST ADDICTING GAMES WE CARRY. IT ALSO KEEPS THE TOP 50 SCORES, AND IS VERY COLORFUL.
AVAILABLE IN KEYBOARD OR JOYSTICK VERSIONS.
CG034 ----- DODGECARS ----- $9.99

TANK

TANK IS A TWO PLAYER SHOOT'EM UP, BATTLE GAME. EACH PLAYER IS AT THE CONTROLS OF A TANK, AND THEIR MISSION IS TO DESTROY THE ENEMY AT ANY COSTS. THIS GAME FEATURES SEVEN DIFFERENT PLAYFIELDS TO BATTLE ON.
AVAILABLE IN KEYBOARD VERSION ONLY.
CG028 ----- TANK ----- $9.99

BANK ROBBERS

FOR ALL YOU WOULD-BE BANK ROBBERS WE OFFER THIS GAME. YOUR PARTNERS ARE ON THE ROOF OF THE BANK THROWING MONEY DOWN TO YOU. YOU'VE GOT TO CATCH AS MUCH AS YOU CAN AND STUFF IT IN THE TRUNK OF YOUR CAR BEFORE THE COPS ARRIVE AND DRAG YOU OFF TO JAIL.
AVAILABLE IN KEYBOARD OR JOYSTICK VERSIONS.
CG038 ----- BANK ROBBERS ----- $9.99

ALIEN PANIC

IN THIS ARCADE TYPE GAME YOU ARE IN A RACE AGAINST TIME AS YOU RACE UP AND DOWN LADDERS, DIGGING TRAPS WHILE AVOIDING THE ALIENS.
AVAILABLE IN KEYBOARD OR JOYSTICK VERSIONS.
CG008 ----- ALIEN PANIC ----- $9.99

COLLIDE

THIS EARLY CLASSIC IS STILL VERY POPULAR BECAUSE OF ITS FAST ACTION, AND THE FACT THAT IT'S FUN TO PLAY. YOU PICK LANES QUICKLY AND CAREFULLY AS YOU RUN OVER DOTS TRYING TO AVOID THE COMPUTER CONTROLLED HAPPY FACE.
AVAILABLE IN KEYBOARD OR JOYSTICK VERSIONS.
CG026 ----- COLLIDE ----- $9.99

MOTOCROSS

WHEN THE GATE DROPS YOU HAD BETTER BE READY, BECAUSE THE ACTION BEGINS QUICKLY. YOU MUST GUIDE YOUR MOTORCYCLE AROUND THE TRACK AVOIDING ROCKS AND HITTING JUMPS TO PICK UP TIME. THIS GAME FEATURES FAST ACTION AND NOVICE OR EXPERT LEVELS.
AVAILABLE IN KEYBOARD OR JOYSTICK VERSIONS.
CG018 ----- MOTOCROSS ----- $9.99

This initial line-up contained several games written by my brother Steve Elder, Bank Robbers and Motocross (above) were among them. He later started a company called Wunderware, selling a lot of Vic 20 games.

The rest of the games were written by me, with a couple exceptions later where we published them on a royalty basis for other authors.

ESCAPE

THIS IS ONE GAME THAT YOU JUST WON'T BELIEVE WITHOUT SEEING IT. THE COMPUTER DRAWS A MAZE (TOTALLY RANDOM FOR AN INFINITE NUMBER OF MAZES) THEN DISPLAYS WHERE YOU ARE AT IN THE MAZE, AND SHOWS YOU WHERE THE EXIT IS. BUT NOW COMES THE INCREDIBLE PART! THE SCREEN THEN CLEARS AND SHOWS YOU THE VIEW OF THE MAZE FROM GROUND LEVEL. FULL 3D GRAPHICS ALLOW YOU TO SEE WAY OFF IN THE DISTANCE. WHEN YOU ARE MOVING, IT SHOWS WALLS COMING CLOSER AND CLOSER, JUST LIKE YOU ARE WALKING AROUND IN A MAZE. IF YOU DO MANAGE TO GET SO LOST THAT THERE'S NO HOPE, THEN YOU CAN HIT THE "C" KEY (FOR CHEAT), AND IT WILL DRAW AN OVERHEAD VIEW OF THE MAZE. A MUST FOR ANY VIC OWNER, THIS GAME WILL SHOW WHAT YOUR COMPUTER IS CAPABLE OF.
AVAILABLE IN KEYBOARD VERSION ONLY.
CG066 ----- ESCAPE ----- $9.99

BLOWUP

YOUR JOB IS SIMPLY TO GET AS MUCH BOOTY AS YOU CAN. DID WE SAY SIMPLE? THROW IN BOMBS, BARRIERS, AND PROGRESSIVELY HARDER SCREENS AND YOU'VE GOT A GAME THAT'S A REAL CHALLENGE. KEEPS HIGH SCORE.
AVAILABLE IN KEYBOARD OR JOYSTICK VERSIONS.
CG006 ----- BLOWUP ----- $9.99

INTERFERENCE IV

YOU'RE CAPTAIN OF THE STARFIGHTER INTERFERENCE IV. YOUR ASSIGNED MISSION IS TO PROTECT YOUR MOTHERSHIPS AS THEY TRAVEL THROUGH YOUR SECTOR, SCORING POINTS FOR THE ASTEROIDS YOU BLAST AWAY.
AVAILABLE IN JOYSTICK VERSION ONLY.
CG062 ----- INTERFERENCE IV ----- $9.99

SIX GUNNER

IF YOU KNOW SOMEONE THAT YOU ALWAYS WANTED TO SHOOT JUST INVITE HIM OVER TO PLAY A GAME OF THIS. SIX GUNNER ALLOWS YOU TO SHOOT THAT PERSON TIME AND TIME AGAIN, WITHOUT THE MESS, OR THE FEAR OF THE GAS CHAMBER.
AVAILABLE IN KEYBOARD VERSION ONLY.
CG052 ----- SIX GUNNER -----$9.99

IT'S A LIVING

YOU'RE AN ASSEMBLY LINE WORKER IN A NUCLEAR WEAPONS FACTORY. YOU'RE IN CHARGE OF FOUR CONVEYORS FULL OF BOMBS. THE BOMBS COME OUT FASTER AND FASTER AS THE GAME PROGRESSES. DON'T LET A BOM HIT THE FLOOR. GREAT GRAPHICS. KEEPS HIGH SCORE.
AVAILABLE IN KEYBOARD OR JOYSTICK VERSIONS.
CG064 ----- IT'S A LIVING ----- $9.99

SEARCH

IN THIS FAST ACTION GAME YOU DRIVE A CAR AROUND A GIANT MAZE OF ROOMS. YOUR GOAL IS TO PICK UP AS MUCH MONEY AS YOU CAN WHILE REMEMBERING WHERE FUEL PUMPS ARE, SO THAT YOU CAN GAS UP WHEN YOU START RUNNING LOW. AS IF RUNNING OUT OF FUEL WASN'T ENOUGH OF A PROBLEM, WE ADDED THE BLOB. WHAT YOU ASK IS THE BLOB? WELL IT'S KIND OF LIKE A GIANT MOVING OIL SLICK THAT IF YOU HIT IT, IT'LL SLIP AND SLIDE YOU BACK TO WHERE YOU STARTED. AVAILABLE IN KEYBOARD OR JOYSTICK VERSIONS.
CG056 ----- SEARCH ----- $9.99

EXECUTIONER

REMEMBER HANGMAN? THIS IS A NEW TWIST! THE NOOSE IS REPLACED BY A GUILLOTINE. MUCH NEATER AND SWIFTER. VERY COLORFUL! EXECUTIONER COMES WITH TWO SETS OF WORDS FOR A TOTAL OF OVER 500 WORDS.
AVAILABLE IN KEYBOARD VERSION ONLY.
CE102 ----- EXECUTIONER ----- $9.99

TALLY

A CLASSIC NUMBER GAME, TALLY IS PLAYED BY TWO PLAYERS OR BY ONE PLAYER AGAINST THE COMPUTER. THIS GAME REQUIRES STRATEGY AND CONCENTRATION. YOU TRY TO SCORE THE HIGH NUMBERS WHILE FORCING YOUR OPPONENT TO SCORE LOW. IT'S VERY ADDICTING.
AVAILABLE IN KEYBOARD VERSION ONLY.
CE104 ----- TALLY ----- $9.99

SPELIT

IF YOU WANT A SPELLING GAME THIS IS THE ONE. THE COMPUTER SHAKES UP THE LETTERED CUBES AND THEN PRESENTS YOU WITH 64 LETTERS THAT YOU MUST FIND WORDS IN. SPELIT CAN PLAY UP TO TWENTY PLAYERS AT A TIME, MAKING IT AN IDEAL FAMILY GAME. THIS ONE WILL BOGGLE YOUR MIND.
KEYBOARD VERSION ONLY.
CE106 ----- SPELIT ----- $9.99

JOURNEY

YOU'RE ON A JOURNEY INTO THE DEPTHS OF A CAVERN WHERE NO ONE HAS EVER BEEN. YOU MUST DODGE THE ROCK FORMATIONS AND COLLECT FUEL AS YOU GO. FAST ACTION AND PLEASING GRAPHICS MAKES THIS A MUST FOR YOU GAME LIBRARY.
AVAILABLE IN KEYBOARD OR JOYSTICK VERSIONS.
CG042 ----- JOURNEY ----- $9.99

We had a lot of games for this initial catalog. Games would only take a few around-the-clock days to write back then, as the Vic 20 had such limited memory, so games had to be compact and to the point, not much room for fluff.

Computer magazines were also just ramping up in popularity. Titles like Creative Computing and Compute! published games that users would type in on their home computers, so we wanted to do the same and give one away in the catalog. It really was all about fun.

```
N-CRSR DOWN
N-CRSR RIGHT
N-CRSR LEFT
J-CLEAR SCREEN
S-HOME
S-REVERSE ON
S-REVERSE OFF
S-BLACK
N-RED
N-YELLOW
N-GREEN
J-BLUE
```

MIMIC is a memory game played by one person. The computer will start by flashing one large number on the screen. The player then presses the key which corresponds with that number. If correct, the computer then flashes the first number followed by a second number. The player then presses those keys in order. Play continues in that manner until the decided upon number of turns has been reached. The player loses when he has guessed wrong three times.

```
1 PRINT"JXMMIMIC (C)1982 NUFEKOP"
2 V=36878:POKEV+1,25:POKEV,15:DIMA(100):X=RND(-TI)
3 A$(1)="..."
4 A$(2)="..."
5 A$(3)="..."
6 A$(4)="..."
7 PRINT"XXXXHOW MANY TURNS-":INPUT"(1 TO 100)";G
8 IFG<1ORG>100THEN7
9 PRINT"J":FORX=1TO100:A(X)=INT(RND(1)*4+1):NEXT:GOTO12
10 PRINT"XXXWRONG!":FORT=1TO1000:NEXT:PRINT"J"
11 IFE=3THEN30
12 Q=Q+1:IFQ=G+1THEN27
13 PRINT"X MY TURN":FORT=1TO1000:NEXT:PRINT"J"
14 FORX=1TOQ:PRINTA$(A(X)):POKEV-2,A(X)*10+150
15 Y=1000-30*Q:IFY<400THENY=400
16 FORT=1TOY:NEXT
17 POKEV-2,0:PRINT"J":FORT=1TO300:NEXT:NEXT
18 PRINT"XX YOUR TURN."
19 POKE198,0:FORX=1TOQ
20 GETI$:I=VAL(I$)
21 IFI<1ORI>4THEN20
22 PRINTA$(I)
23 IFI<>A(X)THENPOKEV-4,130:FORT=1TO200:NEXT:Q=Q-1:E=E+1:POKEV-4,0:GOTO10
24 POKEV-2,I*10+150:FORT=1TO500:NEXT:PRINT"J"
25 POKEV-2,0:NEXT
26 PRINT"XX"Q:FORT=1TO1000:NEXT:GOTO12
27 FORX=1TO5:FORY=1TO4
28 PRINTA$(Y):POKEV-2,Y*10+150:FORT=1TO100:NEXT:POKEV-2,0:PRINT"JXYOU WON!"
29 NEXT:NEXT:POKEV-2,0:GOTO31
30 PRINT"JXXXXYOU BLEW IT!"
31 PRINT"XXXXXXXXPRESS'F1'KEY TO     XPLAY AGAIN."
32 IFPEEK(197)=39THENRUN
33 GOTO32

READY.
```

COMING SOON:

NUFEKOP GAMES FOR ATARI AND SINCLAIR COMPUTERS! WATCH OUR ADS!

KNOCKOUT

HERE'S A VERY GOOD VERSION OF AN OLD CLASSIC COMPUTER GAME. YOU CONTROL A PADDLE THAT BOUNCES A BALL INTO A BRICK WALL, KNOCKING OUT A BRICK EACH TIME IT HITS. VERY COLORFUL GRAPHICS. THIS GAME ALSO FEATURES A TWO PLAYER OPTION, WHERE PLAYERS ALTERNATE TURNS.
AVAILABLE IN KEYBOARD OR JOYSTICK VERSIONS.
CG068 ----- KNOCKOUT ----- $9.99

IN APRIL

WE HAVE 8K GAMES COMING FOR YOUR VIC. THESE WILL INCLUDE SOME ALL NEW TITLES AND SOME EXTENDED VERSIONS OF SOME GAMES THAT ARE PRESENTLY AVAILABLE IN 5K VERSIONS. ALSO COMING ARE GAMES USING ATARI STYLE GAME PADDLES.

MISC.

CASSETTE TAPES

THESE HIGH QUALITY DATA TAPES ARE A MUST FOR SERIOUS PROGRAMMERS. THESE C10 TAPES (5 MINUTES PER SIDE) COME WITH A HARD CASE. MINIMUM ORDER OF 5 TAPES. CALL FOR PRICES ON QUANTITIES OVER 40.
NA204 ----- CASSETTE TAPE ----- $1.00 each

SCREEN CHARTS

TIRED OF GUESS WORK? THESE CHARTS COME IN TABLET FORM, WITH 50 PAGES TO A TABLET. EACH SHEET HAS THREE GRAPHS OF THE STANDARD (8K AND UNDER) VIC SCREEN, AND HAVE ONE GRAPH OF THE COLOR SCREEN. WE CANNOT STRESS ENOUGH, THE HELP THAT THESE ARE TO PROGRAMMING. YOU CAN DRAW WHAT YOU WANT THE SCREEN TO LOOK LIKE ON THESE TABLETS, AND THEN YOU HAVE ALL THE NUMBERS RIGHT IN FRONT OF YOU WHEN YOU WRITE THE PROGRAM. THESE ARE USED BY ALL OF NUFEKOPS AUTHORS WITH VERY PLEASING RESULTS.
NA202 ----- SCREEN REFERENCE CHARTS ----- $4.50 per tablet of 50

We had to source inexpensive cassettes for this business, so after finding them, we also offered them for sale. At this time, blank cassettes were the choice for music and were selling for three or four dollars, we were able to sell them for a dollar and still make a little money on them.

Our order blank. Amazingly crude, we even made them pick if they wanted the game to be controlled from the keyboard or from a joystick. It seemed like the right thing to do at the time. I *think* life was simpler back then, not really sure.

NÜFEKOP P.O. Box 156 Shady Cove, OR 97539				
Name: (Please Print)				
Address:				
City/State: , Zip:				
Phone: ( ) -				
Title	Catalog No.	stick or keys	Quan.	Price
Foriegn Orders Add Shipping				
			TOTAL $	

Policies

PRICES OF TAPES INCLUDE SHIPPING COSTS FOR ORDERS MADE WITHIN THE U.S.. FOREIGN ORDERS REQUIRE $1.50 PER TAPE FOR SHIPPING. THERE IS A SPACE PROVIDED ON THE ORDER BLANK FOR YOU TO SPECIFY EITHER KEYBOARD CONTROL OR ATARI JOYSTICK CONTROL. IF NOT SPECIFIED, WE WILL SHIP THE KEYBOARD VERSION OF THE PROGRAM.

CALL NUFEKOP AT (503)878-2113 TO PLACE C.O.D. ORDERS. CALLS SHOULD BE MADE BETWEEN 9:00 a.m. AND 6:00 p.m.. IF AT ALL POSSIBLE, C.O.D. ORDERS WILL BE SHIPPED THE SAME DAY AS THEY WERE RECEIVED.

ALL OUR PROGRAMS ARE GUARANTEED TO LOAD OR WE WILL GLADLY EXCHANGE IT FOR ONE THAT WILL. ALL OUR TAPES ARE COMPUTER ORIGINALS AND SHOULD ALWAYS LOAD PROPERLY, BUT THERE IS ALWAYS A CHANCE THAT ONE WILL SLIP BY US THAT HAS A DEFECT ON THE TAPE OR SOME OTHER UNFORSEEN PROBLEM. REMEMBER THAT ALL OUR GAMES ARE TAPED TWICE(ONCE ON EACH SIDE), SO TRY BOTH SIDES BEFORE ASSUMING THAT THE TAPE IS BAD. BUT IF YOU DO HAVE A TAPE THAT WILL NOT LOAD, SIMPLY RETURN THE TAPE TO US WITHIN THIRTY DAYS OF PURCHASE AND WE WILL REPLACE IT WITH ANOTHER COPY OF THE SAME PROGRAM.

Getting Started.

We ran some small ads in Compute! magazine and the catalog requests and orders began pouring in. At this point I still worked in my bedroom, there was no office. That would soon change as inventory, packing and shipping needs would dictate.

Here's my old bedroom. The funny thing was, back then having three or four computers and monitors was nearly unheard of and it surprised people that saw it. Now workstations are so common-place, this seems a bit laughable.

Gluing up boxes was a never ending task. There was always a hot glue gun on and ready to burn someone.

We tried all sorts of adhesives but nothing worked as well as hot glue.

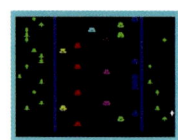

14

Here's a later picture of the "lab" set up in the Nüfekop warehouse. Some development was done here but it was mostly for testing and quality control of products.

Notice the Atari computer sitting there, we were trying to get into the Atari 400/800 market but never quite made it.

Programming was so different and time consuming I never really developed any marketable software for it.

The truth is every time I sat down at an Atari 800, I started playing Space Invaders or Missile Command and didn't get much programming actually done.

Here's an old picture right after getting my first Vic 20. We had a very low serial numbered machine.

Notice the old OSI Challenger 2P computer sitting there. Nice monitor!

16

1BDF INC $1DF0
1BE2 LDA #$FF
1BE4 CMP $1DF0
1BE7 BNE $1B84
1BE9 LDA #$00
VOICE OF:
GARY ELDER
"Nufekop Games"
NUFEKOP

The Hardware.

The Vic 20, C-64, 1701 monitor, Datasette tape deck and 1541 floppy drive. They sold a LOT of these!

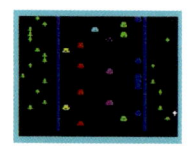

To understand how limited the hardware was in those days, picture this:

A normal icon on your pc desktop is 32 pixels wide by 32 pixels tall and is likely in 24 bit color mode.

That means it takes 32 x 32 x (24/8) bytes to hold the raw image of the icon. It's 3072 bytes, or 3K.

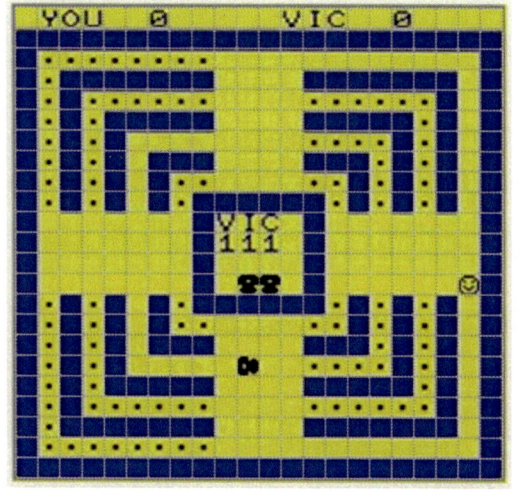

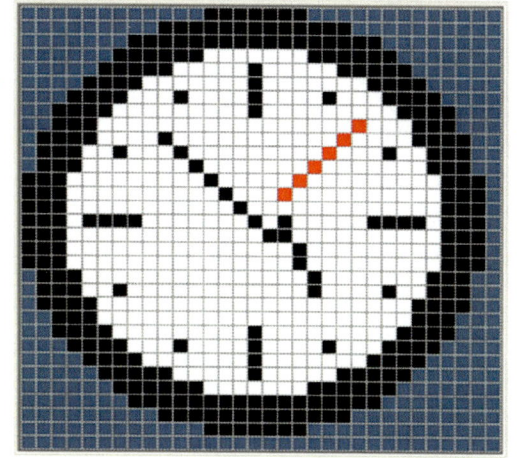

A Vic 20 screen had 22 columns and 23 rows. It took 2 bytes per cell, one byte for the character code, one for the color.

So it's whole screen took 22 x 23 x 2, or 1012 bytes which is just under 1k.

Your single modern icon picture takes three times the space of a whole Vic 20 screen. Not too bad, it proves the Vic was pretty economical with it's ram usage.

The real problem though was the entire Vic 20 had only 3.5k of ram, and the .5k was nearly always consumed holding a custom character set. So you were left with the space of one modern day icon to write all your code, hold all your screens and do your sound effects. Fun, but it always kept you thinking small.

19

Graphics programming on the Vic, particularly on a standard 3k machine was usually done by modifying the character set. The character set is made up of drawings that represent all the characters that can show on the screen.

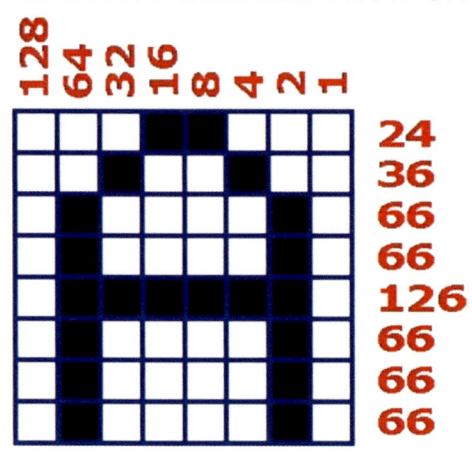

Here is the letter "A". It's made up of several dots or "Pixels". The character is eight pixels wide which allows each row to be held in one byte. There are eight rows, so each character takes eight bytes to store it.

The numbers at the top are the values of each column. You simply add up each "ON" pixel in the row to get that rows value. For example the first row has a byte value of 24, because pixel 8 and pixel 16 are on.

So to do game graphics, you could reshape characters using your own byte values.

Here we've made a ball shape that we want to roll across the screen. If we take those values and put them in memory where the "A" is stored, we'll change the look of the "A" character.

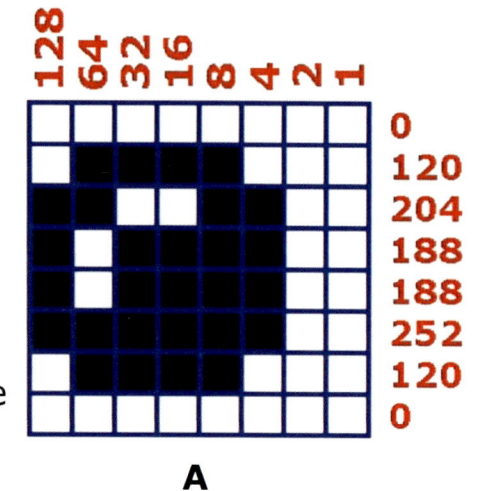

A

Here's part of the screen as it looks at bootup time, with a single "A" character typed in.

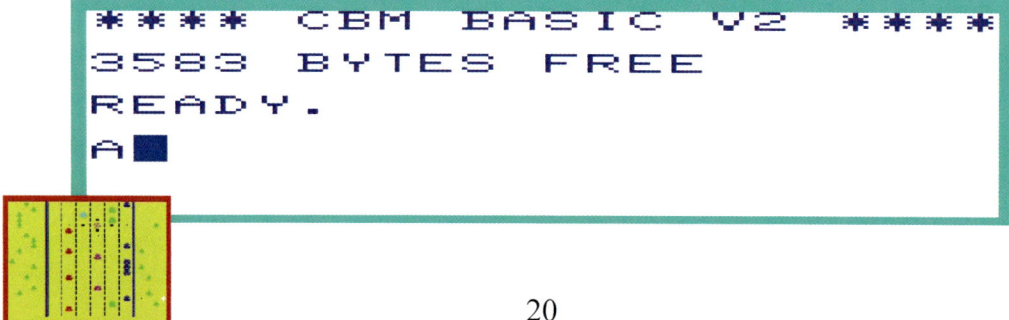

```
**** CBM BASIC V2 ****
3583 BYTES FREE
READY.
A█
```

20

Now if we install our values in place of the "A" values, the screen will now look like this.

Notice how it changed all of the "A" characters to our ball. That's because we've told this system to draw our ball anytime it draws an "A". We could now move our ball by moving the "A" character around the screen. Generally you would write a little code to read the joystick port, see if the player was moving a direction, and move the ball accordingly.

That type of movement only lets you move a whole character cell at a time. To do some finer steps of movement, we'd define more characters, like these below.

We'll build this one and assign it to the letter "B". Notice it's very similar to the one we changed the "A" to, only it's moved the whole ball shape a couple pixels to the right.

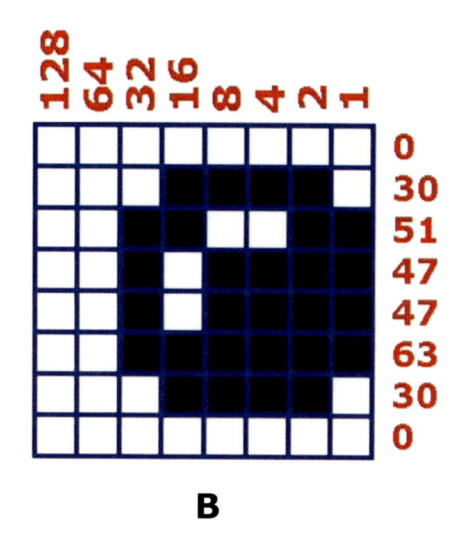

B

Next, we'll do two more characters, the "C" and "D" letters. Again, it's the same ball, just shifted to the right two more pixels. Now the ball doesn't fit in one character, so we put the first part in "C", and put the rest in the "D" character.

	128	64	32	16	8	4	2	1	
									0
					■	■			7
				■	■		■		12
				■		■	■		11
				■		■	■		11
				■	■	■	■		15
					■	■	■		7
									0

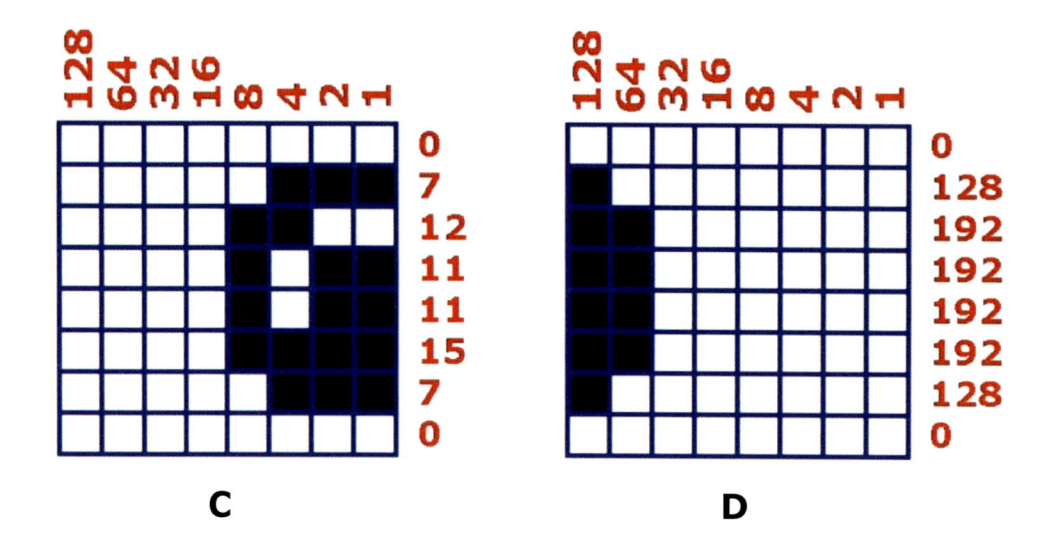

C

	128	64	32	16	8	4	2	1	
									0
	■								128
	■	■							192
	■	■							192
	■	■							192
	■	■							192
	■								128
									0

D

Finally, two more characters, we'll map "E" & "F" to pictures of the ball shifted two more pixels right.

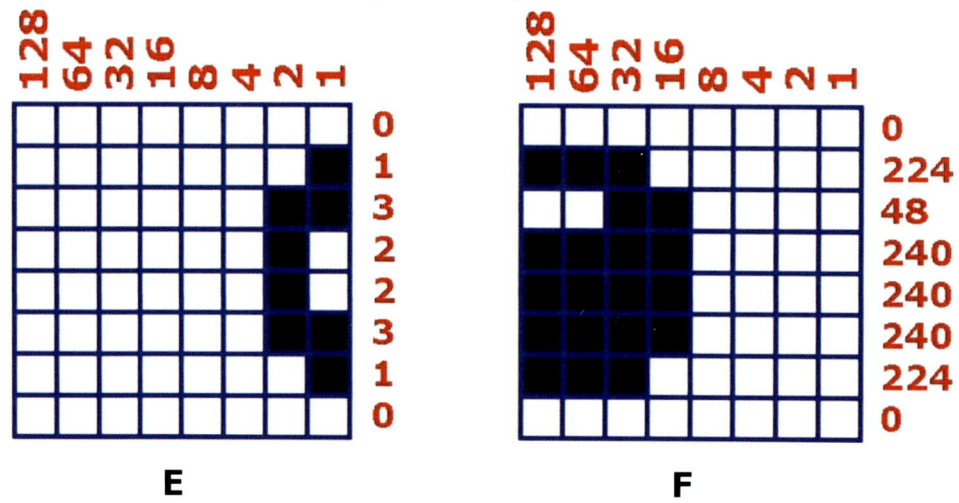

	128	64	32	16	8	4	2	1	
									0
								■	1
							■	■	3
							■		2
							■		2
							■	■	3
								■	1
									0

E

	128	64	32	16	8	4	2	1	
									0
	■	■	■						224
			■	■					48
	■	■	■	■					240
	■	■	■	■					240
	■	■	■	■					240
	■	■	■						224
									0

F

Much like cartoon animation, we've just built the animation frames that when played back properly, will let the ball slide in two pixel increments. That will provide very smooth animation on a Vic. The animation is done by displaying an "A", which is just the ball in it's left position. Next frame, we display the "B" which shows the ball moved slightly to the right.
Next frame, we display a "C" with a "D" right next to it, which moves the ball two more pixels. We then display the "E" & "F" characters and the ball moves to it's final animation position. For the next frame, you start over by displaying the "A", but you now move it one screen position right.

Here is the screen with all the characters that we're going to change, before we install our character set.

```
**** CBM BASIC V2 ****
3583 BYTES FREE
READY.
A  B  CD EF  ■
| | | | | | | | | | |
```

After we install our characters, the same screen looks like this.

```
****   ◖◗M  ◖◗SI◖ V2  ****
3583  ◗YT ◖S  ◗R ◖ ◖
R ◖◗◗ Y.
◗   ◗   ◗    ◗   ■
| | | | | | | | | | |
```

Can you follow what all just happened?
The red lines mark the screen columns so you can see how the letters are all on even boundaries, but our custom characters bleed from one character to another seemingly crossing the cell boundaries. Here are the steps again.

1) We poke an "A" in screen cell position 1

2) Now poke a "B" in cell 1

3) Now a "C" in cell 1, a "D" in cell 2

4) Next poke an "E" in cell 1, a "F" in cell 2

5) Now we put a space in cell 1 to clear it, and an "A" in cell 2. Now you just start repeating the steps using cells 2 and 3, then 3 & 4 and so forth. Are you ready to start programming?

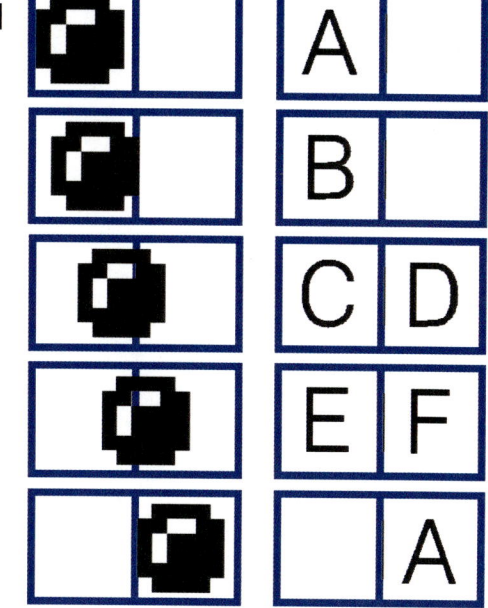

Here's a Vic opened up.
A 6502 processor, a separate 6560 graphics chip, serial port, game controller port and a cartridge port. They actually had 5k of ram, but 1.5k was used by the computer itself, leaving 3.5 available to use. It was fairly common to have your development tools on a cartridge, leaving most of the ram free for your program.

Coding on the Vic could be done using the built-in basic, or if you were really ambitious you could hand write machine language code and enter it a byte at a time. Later there were assemblers that simplified machine language programming.

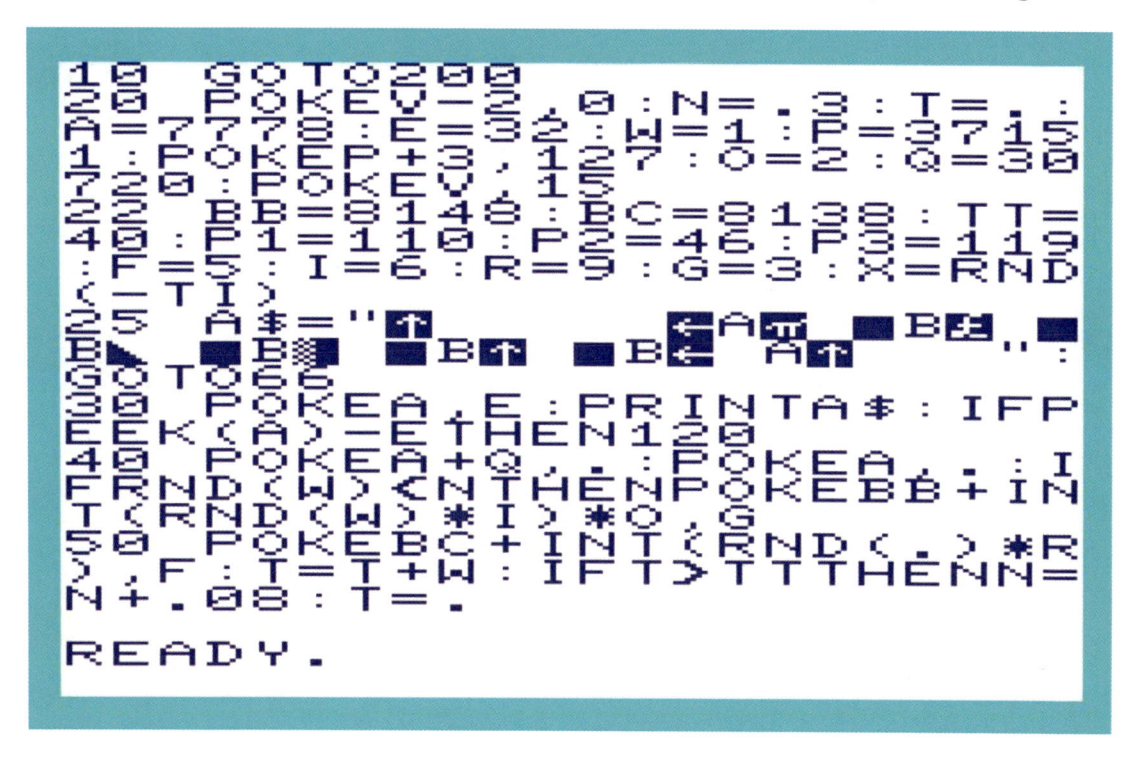

```
10 GOTO200
20 POKEV-2,0:N=.3:T=.:
A=7778:E=32:W=1:P=3715
1:POKEP+3,127:O=2:Q=30
720:POKEV,15
22 BB=8140:BC=8138:TT=
40:P1=110:P2=46:P3=119
:F=5:I=6:R=9:G=3:X=RND
(-TI)
25 A$="▮ ▮B▮ ▮B▮ ▮B▮▮▮▮▮BE.. ▮
B▮ ▮B▮ ▮B▮ ▮":
GOTO66
30 POKEA,E:PRINTA$:IFP
EEK(A)=ETHEN120
40 POKEA+Q,.:POKEA,.:I
FRND(W)<NTHENPOKEBB+IN
T(RND(W)*I)*O,G
50 POKEBC+INT(RND(.)*R
),F:T=T+W:IFT>TTTHENN=
N+.08:T=.

READY.
```

Let's take a look at a little basic code out of Dodgecars and I'll try to explain why this code isn't as bad as it first appears.

First line of code sends execution to some startup code much later in the program. That's good practice on a vic because low numbered lines executed faster, so you would always put your main game code with as low of line numbers as possible and then just step over it with the first line of code.

Now you might be saying, Why is there so many statements on each line. Wouldn't it be much more readable to separate things? Yes, yes it would. It also would take many more bytes. You didn't even use spaces because each space took another byte. Everything was about saving space or time. On line 50, "T=.", Looks flakey, but it was faster than "T=0", which is what it did. Basic was kind of funny, even back then.

Packaging.

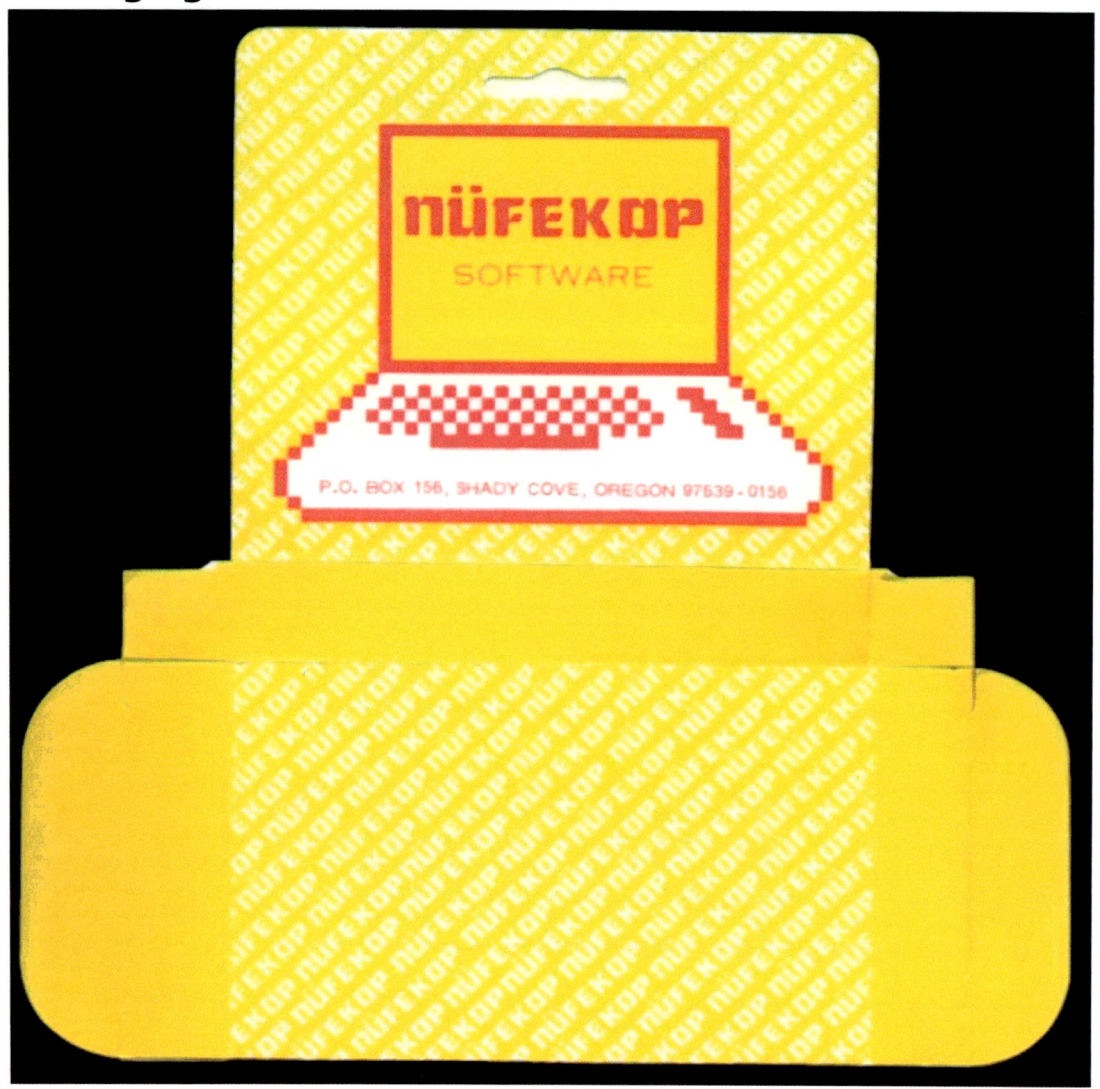

Our original packaging was generic and had labels placed on the front to indicate what game was inside.

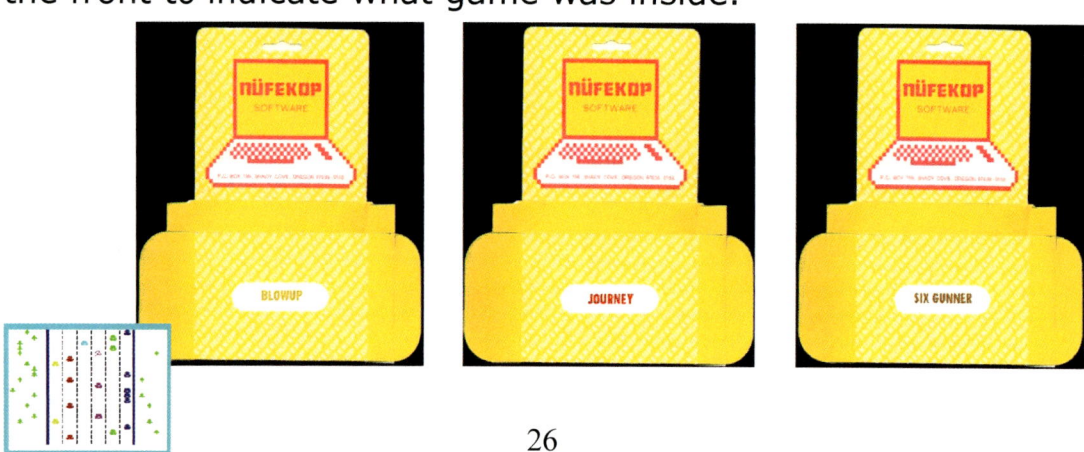

26

We had rubber stamps with all the game names on them.

The local "Rubber Stamp Lady" knew us well from all the frequent visits.

We used them on the front of our original packaging, on the cassette labels, inventory racks, outgoing packages and anything else within walking distance of the stamp pad.

Eventually we phased them out as we did more custom printing.

The next version of packaging had custom printed graphics for most games, though we ran a few blanks that could be rubber stamped for low production titles.

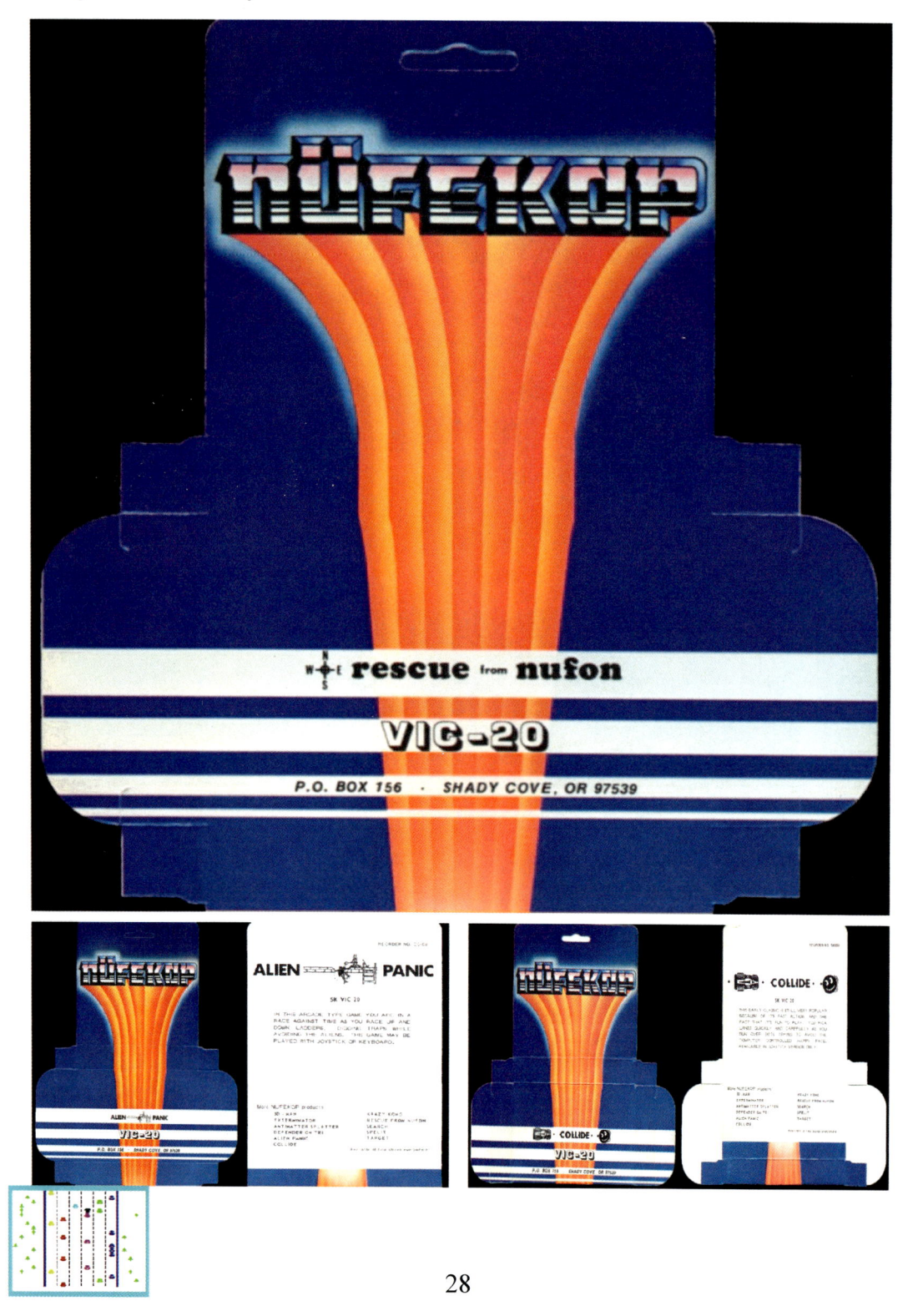

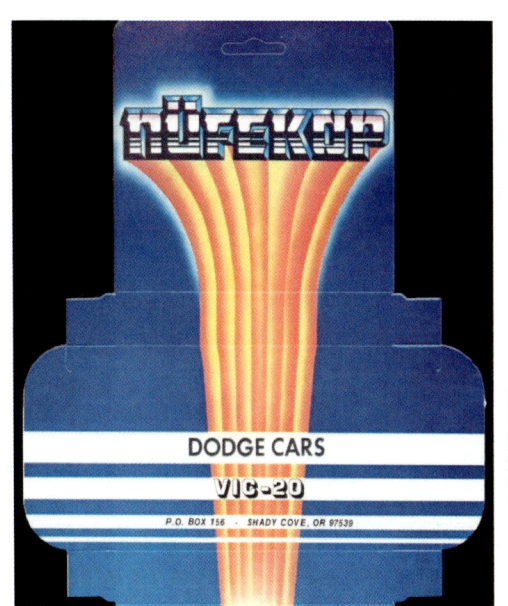

DODGE CARS
5K VIC 20

IF YOU HAVE EVER WONDERED WHAT IT WOULD BE LIKE TO BE GOING THE WRONG WAY ON A FREEWAY THEN YOU REALLY OUGHT TO TRY THIS GAME. YOU MUST DODGE THE EVER-INCREASING TRAFFIC WITH THE HOPE THAT YOU CAN STAY ALIVE JUST A LITTLE LONGER. THE FAST, SMOOTH ACTION OF THIS GAME MAKES IT ONE OF THE MOST ADDICTING GAMES WE CARRY. IT ALSO KEEPS THE TOP 50 SCORES, AND IS VERY COLORFUL. AVAILABLE IN JOYSTICK VERSION ONLY.

More NUFEKOP products!
- 3D - MAN
- EXTERMINATOR
- ANTIMATTER SPLATTER
- DEFENDER ON TRI
- ALIEN PANIC
- COLLIDE
- KRAZY KONG
- RESCUE FROM NUFON
- SEARCH
- SPELIT
- TARGET

Available at fine stores everywhere!

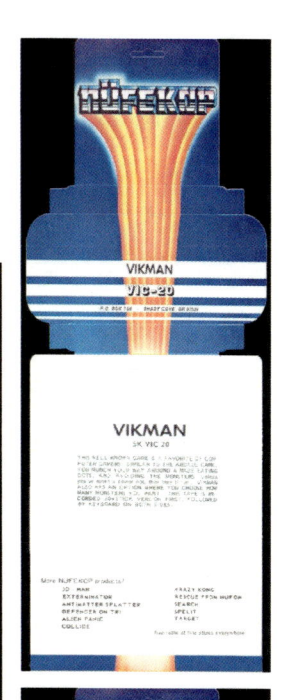

QUIRK
5K VIC 20

FOR YOU PEOPLE WHO CAN'T SIT STILL, THIS IS ONE THAT'LL KEEP YOU HOPPING. BY JUMPING THROUGH HOLES IN THE MOVING FLOORS YOU ATTEMPT TO CATCH FALLING OBJECTS BEFORE THEY HIT THE BOTTOM LEVEL. IF YOU CAN JUMP TO THE TOP FLOOR YOU CAN GET AN ENERGIZER POD THAT INCREASES THE POINTS OF THE PRIZES YOU CATCH. QUICK REACTIONS ARE A MUST IN THIS FAST, ARCADE TYPE GAME. AVAILABLE JOYSTICK VERSION ONLY.

More NUFEKOP products!
- 3D - MAN
- EXTERMINATOR
- ANTIMATTER SPLATTER
- DEFENDER ON TRI
- ALIEN PANIC
- COLLIDE
- KRAZY KONG
- RESCUE FROM NUFON
- SEARCH
- SPELIT
- TARGET

Available at fine stores everywhere!

30

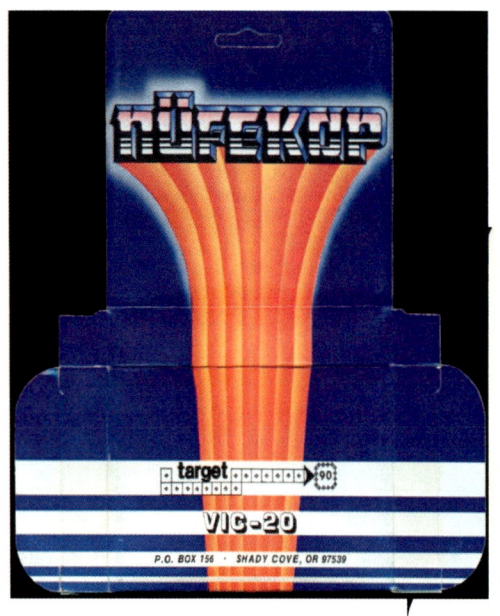

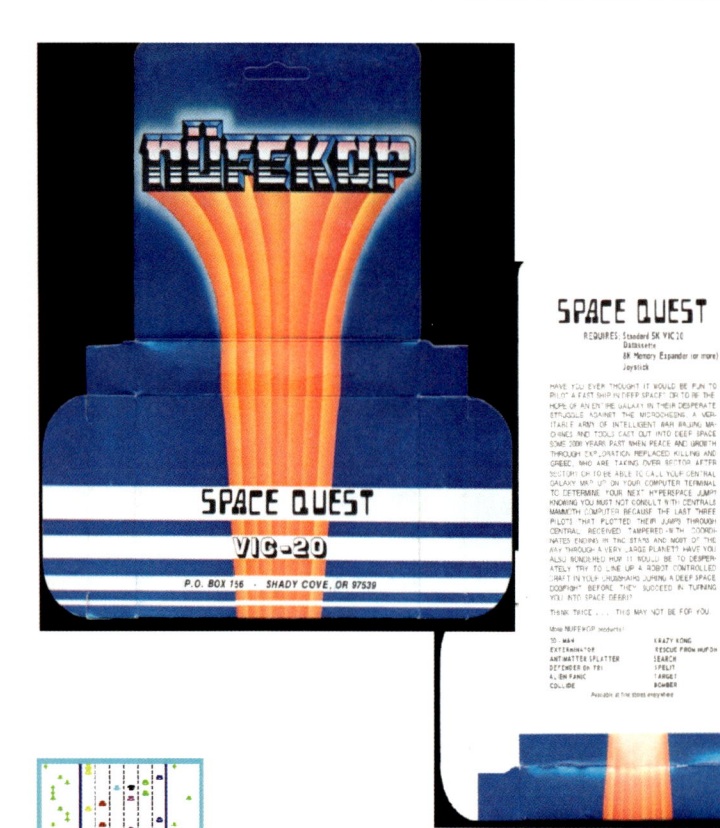

The Instructions.

What would a game be without the obligatory instruction sheet? Most of the time they were a bit of an afterthought, but occasionally a gem would show up, usually written by Gary.

THE THIRTEENH KING

tortured existence for his subjects? It was said he had boasted he had gold enough to buy his place among the GODS themselves. Among the GODS by murder? Among the GODS by causing starvation? Among the GODS by gold?

Tonight we know . . . tonight we witnessed fulfillment of a pact 'tween man and immortal . . . tonight we glimpsed the blindness of greed, a blindness that caused a powerful man to think himself capable of dealing with GODS.

We knew not what we would find when our ragtag peasant-farmer-merchant army stormed the castle. We knew only of our dead sons and starving wives. The castle soldiers fought spiritlessly, some joining our cause.

We had seen nothing of the king or his companion until we burst the last door, the mammoth door of the royal treasury . . . Every man froze. Blood turned to water then ice in our veins. We watched this blasphemy, powerless even to close our eyes. The king tallied the last of his kingdom's gold and pushed them into a bag held by a DEMON! He was possessed! No man could look upon that creature and speak! After the last coin had fallen into the bag that did not fill, the king declared, "I have fulfilled my share of the bargain. Now you must honor yours. I demand immortality! I demand my place among the GODS!"

The king drew on the better part of his heritage and dignity to speak even in the face of this abomination, as no one else among us could, saying, "monster of me, cannot you bring back those dead by my hand? Do with me as you will, but let me make amends with the people. If you resurrect one thousand, then multiply my tortures by ten times one thousand." The demon was silent for a moment, then said, "There is a way to release everyone from the five levels and it is so difficult and so ironic I shall share it with you. The gold, like the spirits of the sons you murdered, finds no peace in this place you're going, forever rolling and falling around. All you need to do is gather all the gold into this bag whereby it and all involved will be brought back to the very spot we stand". Then, as if having made some monumental joke, he threw back his head and started laughing.

When we awoke, the chamber was empty of all but tables, chairs and us. We broke up into small bands and headed towards our respective villages, laden not with the attitude of victors, but with stories of morality and penalties for the disregard of it.

I for one certainly hope you get the *message.

*There is only one true bargain worth striking . . . This game at $16.95.

The young king's ancestry must be partially at fault", one of them murmured. "He knew nothing but of kings! His father the king, his grandfather the king, his great grandfather the king, twelve generations of kings! The thirteenth generation of absolute power . . . can it be his fault alone he thought himself GOD enough to strike a bargain like this?'" After the speaker's involuntary shudder, silence, broken only by the occasional hiss of the last escaping moisture from glowing embers of the campfire, settled heavily on the men positioned somewhat haphazardly around the glow. It seemed a physical need to turn inward, for each man to evaluate the framework of his innermost sanctuary seeing if damage done by repercussions of that which they had witnessed this day left strength enough for the weight of silence or the press of night.

One man's mind drifted back a year to when the strangeness in the kingdom had just begun. The young prince had always had a eye for gold but after his father died in the hunting accident and, at twenty was declared king, it became an obsession! No family could pay the taxes he imposed without starving . . . and the penalties! He, the oldest son of the royal family himself, would publicly burn at the stake the eldest son of any family thought by him, or his cursed advisor, to be withholding coins rightfully due him. Rumors were about that his advisor was an agent from Hades or some form of a demon. Why would a king create such an impoverished,

The laughter started low, with no focal point. It seemed to be coming from countless voices, from everywhere all at once, as horrible in its' unearthly origin as the look on the demon's face as he spoke, gurgling, deep, terrible to the man now seemingly dwarfed before him, "You speak of, but know not this word 'honor'." Shrieks, near deafening, of laughter then the demon continued, "Fool king! I love you powerful men, you sink so low from places so high. All the better for me! With one omission you have paid the price for immortality, you must see me first as I really am. LOOK UPON ME . . . KING!."

It mattered not that we had come to end his life, we felt nothing but sympathy for the man seeing for the first time the true form of his year-long council. The anguish he felt must have been unbearable, for he dropped to his knees, face ashen. The hoots and screams of laughter had risen in volume until they seemed a tangible, pulsing force when again spoke the demon, "You are immortal now, king. You can never die permanently, as I have been fashioned in your likeness. Yes, greedy thirteenth king, all humankinds, demons and devils are given life by the very one they tempt, so fashioned also is the abode of your newly acquired longevity. From now to eternity you will be condemned to the five levels of your personal Hades, shared by those you have murdered in your quest for the gold coins that meant so much."

Kings Ransom
INSTRUCTIONS

REQUIRED:

Commodore VIC-20 Computer
If tape version: Commodore Cassette Player
If disk version: 1540 or 1541 Disk Drive
Joystick is optional but preferred.

LOADING:

If tape, insert cassette into player and rewind. Press and hold the left hand (SHIFT) key then press and release the (RUN-STOP) key. Release the (SHIFT) key and press (PLAY) on tape deck. The screen should soon display a FOUND and LOADING message.

If disk, after making sure that disk drive is connected and relatively level, insert KINGS RANSOM diskette into drive. Type: LOAD "KINGS RANSOM", 8 then RUN.

KINGS RANSOM INSTRUCTIONS CONTINUED ON NEXT PAGE

KINGS RANSOM INSTRUCTIONS

MOVEMENT:

Right and left movement is controlled by either right and left movements of the joystick or by pressing the Z or C keys. Jumping is caused by pressing the FIRE button on the joystick or the SPACE bar on your computer. Jumping sideways is accomplished by moving sideways then jumping. This allows you to jump over the indeed and even become a real test in your play of the game.

PLAY:

The idea is to run around catching the Gold Coins you sold out his so long ago. They now hold the very hope for escape for you and the countless lost souls condemned along with you to share an eternity of pointless drifting up and down the levels of undeath. The method, whether going down or up, are to be avoided at all costs.

HINTS:

This game, like most of the best arcade style games, seems a little hard when starting out but will, as your feel for it grows, become one of your favorites. Some players were so lured that by staying on the second level down it moves a little slower and will venturing down to lower levels, if they have a clear route to a coin works well. We have seen several routes in excess of 600.

31

The first instruction sheets were very crude, mostly written in my bedroom using an old typewriter. At eighteen years old I was not prone to putting a lot of effort into things like this.

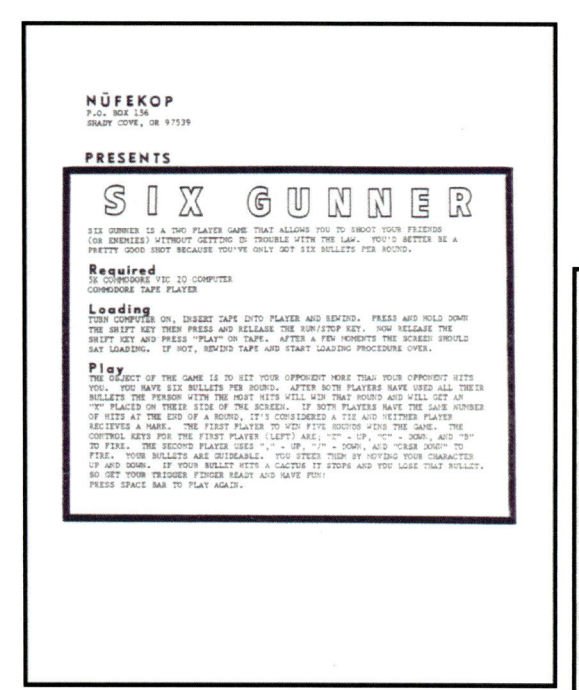

I'm sure there are typo's throughout and don't get me started on proper grammer, I still haven't figured that all out.

Games like Tank required two players, no computer opponent. You and a friend had to share the keyboard at the same time. It shows how eager people were to play, can you imagine doing that today?

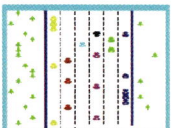

33

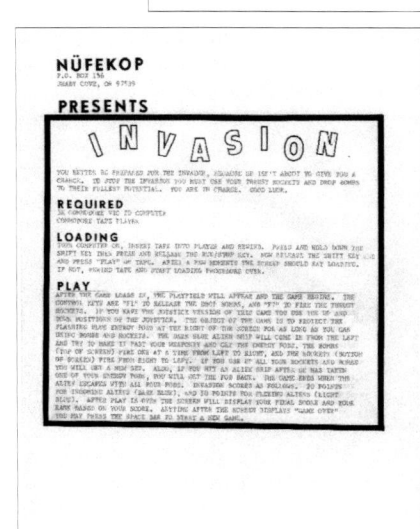

The next round of instructions were much more professional, trying to have a more consistent look. They were still being folded up and slipped in alongside a cassette tape.

hickup

P.O. BOX 158 SHADY COVE, OR 97539

PRESENTS

ALIEN PANIC

IT'S CHASING YOU, RUN . . . . . . NO, IT TURNED AROUND, BUT YOU HAD BETTER NOT REST, YOU'RE FIGHTING AGAINST TIME, SO TURN AROUND AND DIG A TRAP, BUT YOU HAD BEST HURRY, THE ALIEN HAS HIS SIGHTS SET ON YOU!

REQUIRED
5K COMMODORE VIC 20 COMPUTER
COMMODORE TAPE PLAYER

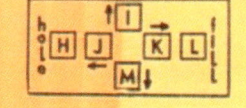

LOADING
TURN COMPUTER ON, INSERT TAPE INTO PLAYER AND REWIND. (ALIEN PANIC IS RECORDED WITH THE KEYBOARD VERSION FOLLOWING THE JOYSTICK VERSION ON BOTH SIDES OF TAPE. TO USE THE KEYBOARD, SET THE FOOT COUNTER TO ZERO AND FAST FORWARD THE TAPE UNTIL IT REACHES 40.) PRESS AND HOLD DOWN THE SHIFT KEY THEN PRESS AND RELEASE THE RUN/STOP KEY. NOW RELEASE THE SHIFT KEY AND PRESS "PLAY" ON TAPE. AFTER A FEW SECONDS THE SCREEN SHOULD SAY LOADING. IF NOT, REWIND TAPE AND START LOADING PROCEDURE OVER.

PLAY
THE IDEA IN "ALIEN PANIC" IS NOT TO.

YOU, BEING ARMED ONLY WITH A SHOVEL, MUST DEMONSTRATE ACCURATE TIMING AND DECISION MAKING TO SURVIVE FOR LONG IN THIS, ABANDONED TO THE ALIENS, CONSTRUCTION SITE.

TO BURY AN ALIEN YOU MUST FIRST DIG THE HOLE. THIS IS DONE BY PRESSING THE FIRE BUTTON AND PULLING BACK ON THE JOYSTICK. THE NEXT STEP IS FILLING IN THE HOLE ON TOP OF THE CREATURE. THIS IS TRICKY AND WHERE TIMING COMES INTO PLAY. STANDING IN THE SAME POSITION YOU WERE IN WHEN DIGGING THE HOLE YOU MUST WAIT UNTIL THE ALIEN FALLS IN. YOU WILL HAVE ONLY SECONDS TO FILL IN OVER THE TOP OF HIM BEFORE HE WORKS HIS WAY OUT OF THE HOLE AND RUNS OVER THE TOP OF YOU! TO FILL, PRESS FIRE BUTTON AND PUSH STICK FORWARD. THIS ALL SOUNDS VERY EASY DOESN'T IT?

SCORE IS A COMPOSITE OF NUMBER OF ALIENS BURIED / TIME IT TOOK TO BURY THEM AND IS DISPLAYED AFTER YOU HAVE LOST ALL YOUR THREE LIVES.

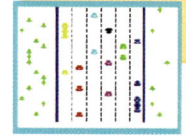

NUKEKOP PRESENTS

★ defender on tri ★

tri city update

tri city update

tri city update

tri city update

directions on tri

loading
INSTALL 3K MEMORY EXPANDER AND TURN COMPUTER ON. INSERT TAPE INTO PLAYER AND REWIND. PRESS AND HOLD SHIFT KEY THEN PRESS AND RELEASE RUN/STOP KEY. NOW RELEASE SHIFT KEY AND PRESS PLAY ON TAPE PLAYER. AFTER A MOMENT THE SCREEN SHOULD SAY LOADING. IF NOT, THEN REPEAT LOADING PROCEDURE.

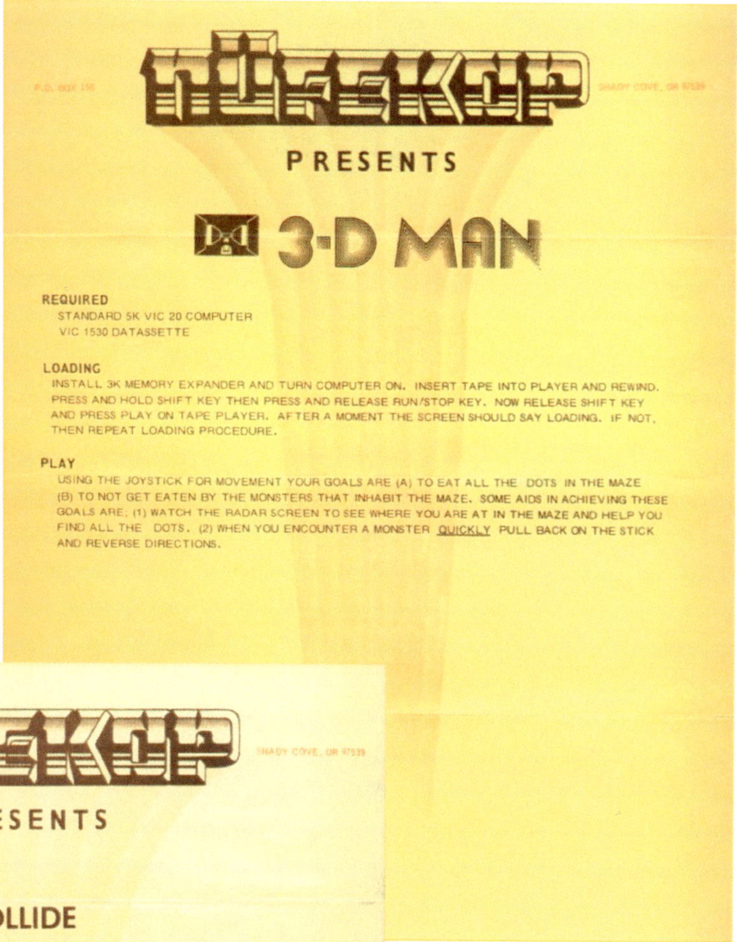

play
SHIELDS ARE ENERGIZED BY PRESSING FIRE BUTTON. TWO COSTS BLASTS OF FUEL EACH TIME, BUT THEY ARE ESSENTIAL TO THE PLAY AS ALIENS' LIGHTNING YOU TOUCH INCLUDING A ZAPPER TRAILED KIT WILL FIRE THE ENERGY SHIELDS ARE ENERGIZED. TO HELP DEFEAT THE ALIENS A CURSOR SHOWN IN THE BLACK STRIP CAN POINT OUT A SEARCHER. BLUE TO RENEW ENERGY SUPPLY YOU'LL FLY YOUR SHIP BY PUSHING THE PULL FUNCTION. IN THE FIRST SCREEN NEAR THE MIDDLE YOU WILL FIND THE FIRST SCIENTIST HANGING FROZEN WITH FEARS, PICK HIM UP BY ZAPPING HIM WITH THE ZAP.
IN THE LOWER RIGHT HAND CORNER OF THE FIRST THREE SCREEN THERE ARE A COUPLE OF RED ARROWS. THESE ARE YOUR COMMAND TO THE NEXT SCREEN AND THE NEXT SET OF OBSTACLES. TO SAVE THE SCIENTIST YOU MUST FLY THE ROYS AT ALIENS NOT IN THE AREA MARKED BAND IN THE FOURTH SCREEN WHERE THEY CAN BE TELEPORTED BACK TO EARTHSHIP. THERE ARE BONUS POINTS FOR EVERY TEN ARRIVAL, BUT YOU ARE NOT AS MANY AS CAN BE HAD BY SAVING ALL THE ALIEN TREASURES TAKE FIRE, BUT ALSO:
HAVING SUCCESSFULLY DROPPED PASSENGER AND CARGO OFF OF IMAGES YOU ARE READY TO MAKE YOUR NEXT TRIAL. TO ACHIEVE THIS LOOK UP ABOVE THE CARGO: YOU WILL SEE A BLACK SQUARE THAT LOOKING LIKE THE SIDE OF YOUR SHIP WILL JUST FIT... 7 DOGS.
A FEW WORDS OF WARNING, THE NEXT TRIP THROUGH DUE TO INCREASING HEAT FROM THE SUN THE MACHINERY WILL BE MOVING TWICE AS FAST.
THE THIRD TRIP WILL HAVE YOU ON THE EDGE OF YOUR PILOT'S SEAT WE THINK.
TO PLAY AGAIN, PRESS FIRE BUTTON.

NUKEKOP
P.O. BOX 136 • SHADY COVE, OR 97539

PRESENTS

3-D MAN

REQUIRED
STANDARD 5K VIC 20 COMPUTER
VIC 1530 DATASSETTE

LOADING
INSTALL 3K MEMORY EXPANDER AND TURN COMPUTER ON. INSERT TAPE INTO PLAYER AND REWIND. PRESS AND HOLD SHIFT KEY THEN PRESS AND RELEASE RUN/STOP KEY. NOW RELEASE SHIFT KEY AND PRESS PLAY ON TAPE PLAYER. AFTER A MOMENT THE SCREEN SHOULD SAY LOADING. IF NOT, THEN REPEAT LOADING PROCEDURE.

PLAY
USING THE JOYSTICK FOR MOVEMENT YOUR GOALS ARE (A) TO EAT ALL THE DOTS IN THE MAZE (B) TO NOT GET EATEN BY THE MONSTERS THAT INHABIT THE MAZE. SOME AIDS IN ACHIEVING THESE GOALS ARE, (1) WATCH THE RADAR SCREEN TO SEE WHERE YOU ARE AT IN THE MAZE AND HELP YOU FIND ALL THE DOTS. (2) WHEN YOU ENCOUNTER A MONSTER <u>QUICKLY</u> PULL BACK ON THE STICK AND REVERSE DIRECTIONS.

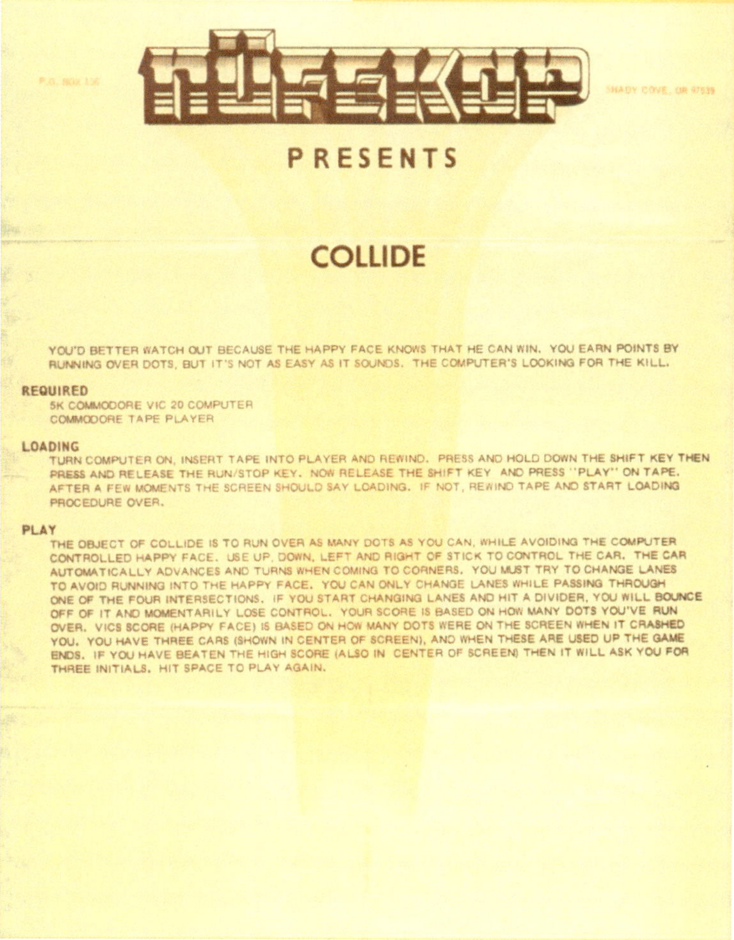

NUKEKOP
P.O. BOX 136 • SHADY COVE, OR 97539

PRESENTS

COLLIDE

YOU'D BETTER WATCH OUT BECAUSE THE HAPPY FACE KNOWS THAT HE CAN WIN. YOU EARN POINTS BY RUNNING OVER DOTS, BUT IT'S NOT AS EASY AS IT SOUNDS. THE COMPUTER'S LOOKING FOR THE KILL.

REQUIRED
5K COMMODORE VIC 20 COMPUTER
COMMODORE TAPE PLAYER

LOADING
TURN COMPUTER ON, INSERT TAPE INTO PLAYER AND REWIND. PRESS AND HOLD DOWN THE SHIFT KEY THEN PRESS AND RELEASE THE RUN/STOP KEY. NOW RELEASE THE SHIFT KEY AND PRESS "PLAY" ON TAPE. AFTER A FEW MOMENTS THE SCREEN SHOULD SAY LOADING. IF NOT, REWIND TAPE AND START LOADING PROCEDURE OVER.

PLAY
THE OBJECT OF COLLIDE IS TO RUN OVER AS MANY DOTS AS YOU CAN, WHILE AVOIDING THE COMPUTER CONTROLLED HAPPY FACE. USE UP, DOWN, LEFT AND RIGHT OF STICK TO CONTROL THE CAR. THE CAR AUTOMATICALLY ADVANCES AND TURNS WHEN COMING TO CORNERS. YOU MUST TRY TO CHANGE LANES TO AVOID RUNNING INTO THE HAPPY FACE. YOU CAN ONLY CHANGE LANES WHILE PASSING THROUGH ONE OF THE FOUR INTERSECTIONS. IF YOU START CHANGING LANES AND HIT A DIVIDER, YOU WILL BOUNCE OFF OF IT AND MOMENTARILY LOSE CONTROL. YOUR SCORE IS BASED ON HOW MANY DOTS YOU'VE RUN OVER. VIC'S SCORE (HAPPY FACE) IS BASED ON HOW MANY DOTS WERE ON THE SCREEN WHEN IT CRASHED YOU. YOU HAVE THREE CARS (SHOWN IN CENTER OF SCREEN), AND WHEN THESE ARE USED UP THE GAME ENDS. IF YOU HAVE BEATEN THE HIGH SCORE (ALSO IN CENTER OF SCREEN) THEN IT WILL ASK YOU FOR THREE INITIALS. HIT SPACE TO PLAY AGAIN.

NUKEKOP

PRESENTS

GALLOWS

REQUIRED
STANDARD COMMODORE VIC 20 COMPUTER
VIC 1530 DATASSETTE (TAPE PLAYER)

LOADING
TURN COMPUTER ON, INSERT TAPE INTO PLAYER AND REWIND. PRESS AND HOLD THE SHIFT KEY, THEN PRESS AND RELEASE THE RUN/STOP KEY. THEN RELEASE THE SHIFT KEY AND PRESS PLAY ON THE TAPE PLAYER. AFTER A MOMENT THE SCREEN SHOULD SAY "LOADING". IF NOT THEN REWIND OR TRY PROCEDURE.

PLAY
TO CHOOSE A WORD RANDOMLY, PRESS DATA. PRESS THE APPROPRIATE NUMBER OF LINES/LETTERS AND MANY WORDS WHEN AT THE PROPER POSITION LINE.
IF A LETTER IS USED MORE THAN ONCE IN THE WORD, IT WILL BE DISPLAYED AT ALL LOCATIONS OR FIRST TRY.

OUR WORDS IN YOUR WORDS
EVERY TIME OF YOUR GALLOWS TAPE IS A FREE STORE PROGRAM CONSISTING OF THE MAKING DISPLAYS AND DRAWING PROGRAM PART OF THE PROGRAM BUT DESCRIBED IN A ROBOT LIST.

TO ENTER YOUR OWN WORDS, LOAD THE LIST INTO YOUR VIC AND LIST THE PROGRAM. STARTING WITH ANY LINE NUMBER HIGHER THAN THE LAST LINE IN OUR PROGRAM ENTER YOUR WORDS AS IN THE LINES FOLLOWING FORMAT:

(NN NUM WORD, WORD, WORD, WORD, ETC.)

AFTER FILLING A LINE WITH WORDS YOU MUST HIT RETURN AND START A NEW LINE WITH A HIGHER LINE NUMBER AND A NEW DATA STATEMENT.

AFTER YOU HAVE ENTERED ALL YOUR WORDS YOU ARE LIMITED ONLY BY AVAILABLE MEMORY. TO FIND OUT HOW MUCH IS LEFT, TYPE: ? FRE (0), THEN CHANGE LINE NUMBER 5 TO READ:

5 ... N=TOTAL NUMBER OF WORDS

AND A SPACE TO BEGIN THE GALLOWS.

NUFEKOP

P.O. BOX 156   SHADY COVE, OR 97539

PRESENTS

RESCUE FROM NÜFON

YOU'RE ON A MISSION TO THE ALIEN BUILDING LOCATED ON THE PLANET NUFON. THERE ARE 30 HUMANS TRAPPED SOMEWHERE IN THE FIVE STORY COMPLEX. YOU MUST LOCATE THE HUMANS, STRAP ON THEIR TELAPORT LOCATERS, AND SIGNAL THE MOTHERSHIP TO BEAM THEM UP. BUT IT'S NOT THAT SIMPLE. THERE ARE FOUR DIFFERENT RACES OF HOSTILE ALIENS THAT YOU MUST AVOID, OR FACE THE POSSIBILITY OF HAVING ALIENS SHOW YOU HOW THEY OVERCAME THE LAST 29 PEOPLE WHO HAVE TRIED TO RESCUE HUMANS FROM NUFON:

REQUIRED
5K COMMODORE VIC 20 COMPUTER
COMMODORE TAPE PLAYER

LOADING
TURN COMPUTER ON, INSERT TAPE INTO PLAYER AND REWIND. PRESS AND HOLD DOWN THE SHIFT KEY THEN PRESS AND RELEASE THE RUN/STOP KEY. NOW RELEASE THE SHIFT KEY AND PRESS "PLAY" ON TAPE. AFTER A FEW MOMENTS THE SCREEN SHOULD SAY LOADING. IF NOT, REWIND TAPE AND START LOADING PROCEDURE OVER. THIS GAME IS IN TWO PARTS, THE INTRO PROGRAM WILL LOAD IN, AND THEN THE MAIN PROGRAM WILL LOAD IN (SELF LOADING). BE SURE AND NOT SHUT THE TAPE OFF UNTIL THE GAME IS IN AND RUNNING.

PLAY
HERE IS A LIST AND SHORT DESCRIPTION OF THE CONTROL KEYS.
"N" – NORTH – MOVES PLAYER NORTH
"S" – SOUTH – MOVES PLAYER SOUTH
"E" – EAST – MOVES PLAYER EAST
"W" – WEST – MOVES PLAYER WEST
"U" – UP – WHEN PLAYER IS IN ELEVATOR, MOVES PLAYER UP ONE LEVEL.
"D" – DOWN – WHEN PLAYER IS IN ELEVATOR, MOVES PLAYER DOWN ONE LEVEL.
"F" – FIRE – FIRES ENERGY WEAPON, USES NEEDED ENERGY.
"T" – TRANSPORT – AFTER PLAYER HAS FOUND HUMAN AND READIED THEM WITH LOCATER, PRESSING THIS WILL SIGNAL THE SHIP TO TRANSPORT HUMAN TO SHIP.

AS SOON AS GAME LOADS IN, PLAY BEGINS. YOU HAVE ALREADY BEAMED DOWN TO THE THIRD FLOOR OF THE BUILDING, SOMEWHERE NEAR THE CENTER OF THE LEVEL. YOU MUST IMMEDIATELY GET TO WORK. THE TIME WILL CONSTANTLY TICK AWAY, REMINDING YOU THAT YOU MUST SUCCEED WITH YOUR MISSION QUICKLY, BECAUSE WHEN THE TIME RUNS OUT THE MOTHERSHIP WILL DESTROY THE ENTIRE PLANET TO PUT AN END TO THE ALIENS REIGN OF TERROR. YOU SEE ONLY ONE ROOM AT A TIME. TO GET TO ANOTHER ROOM, JUST WALK THROUGH ANY OF THE EXITS IN THE WALLS. YOU CAN DESTROY AN ALIEN AT ANY TIME BY FIRING YOUR ENERGY PHASOR. IT WILL EASILY DESTROY AN ALIEN INTO DUST, BUT IT COSTS ENERGY TO DO SO. YOU LOSE BETWEEN 20 AND 40 DEPENDING ON THE SPECIE OF ALIEN. IF AN ALIEN DOES GET TOO CLOSE TO YOU THEN IT IS TO YOUR ADVANTAGE TO FIRE, BECAUSE IT USES LESS ENERGY THAN GETTING HIT BY ONE. WHEN YOU FIND A HUMAN YOU MUST GET CLOSE ENOUGH THAT YOU HEAR A SOUND, AND THEN THE HUMAN WILL CHANGE COLOR SLIGHTLY. THIS MEANS THAT YOU HAVE STRAPPED A LOCATER OUT OF YOUR BACKPACK ON HIM, AND THAT HE CAN NOW BE BEAMED UP. A FEW OTHER THINGS TO KEEP IN MIND ARE: YOU USE A POINT OF ENERGY EVERY STEP, SO MAKE YOUR MOVES WISELY. YOU USE TWENTY POINTS OF ENERGY WHEN YOU GO UP OR DOWN ELEVATORS. YOU WILL KNOW WHEN YOU'RE IN AN ELEVATOR, IT'S PLAINLY MARKED. THE GAME ENDS WHEN YOU HAVE RAN OUT OF TIME AND THE PLANET IS DESTROYED, WHEN YOU HAVE USED ALL YOUR ENERGY, OR IF YOU MANAGE TO COMPLETE THE MISSION OF RESCUEING ALL THE HUMANS. REMEMBER THAT THE BUILDING IS DIFFERENT EVERY GAME, SO EVERY TIME YOU PLAY THE SITUATION IS DIFFERENT. GOOD LUCK...
HIT SPACE BAR TO PLAY AGAIN.

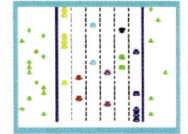

NUFEKOP PRESENTS

ANTIMATTER SPLATTER!

REQUIRED
STANDARD 5K VIC 20 COMPUTER
VIC 1530 DATASSETTE

LOADING
TURN COMPUTER ON, INSERT TAPE AND REWIND. PRESS AND HOLD (SHIFT), THEN PRESS AND RELEASE (RUN/STOP) AND RELEASE (SHIFT). PRESS (PLAY) ON THE TAPE PLAYER. AFTER A MOMENT THE SCREEN WILL SAY "LOADING". IF NOT, REPEAT LOADING PROCEDURE.

PLAY
USING THE (Z) AND (C) KEYS OR THE JOYSTICK TO MOVE YOUR SPLATTER CANNON AND EITHER THE (SHIFT) KEY OR THE FIRE BUTTON ON YOUR JOYSTICK TO FIRE THE SPLATTER MATTER INTO THE ANTI-MATTER CAUSING OF COURSE THE ANTI-MATTER TO SPLATTER AND YOUR SCORE TO GO UP 10 POINTS.

NUFEKOP PRESENTS

ESCAPE

YOU'RE LOST IN A MAZE AND NO IDEA OF WHAT TO DO. ALL YOU SEE ARE LOTS OF ROOMS AND HALLWAYS AND DOORWAYS. CAN YOU FIND THE WAY OUT??

REQUIRED
5K COMMODORE VIC 20 COMPUTER
COMMODORE TAPE PLAYER

LOADING
TURN COMPUTER ON, INSERT TAPE INTO PLAYER AND REWIND. PRESS AND HOLD DOWN THE SHIFT KEY THEN PRESS AND RELEASE THE RUN/STOP KEY. NOW RELEASE THE SHIFT KEY AND PRESS "PLAY" ON TAPE. AFTER A FEW MOMENTS THE SCREEN SHOULD SAY LOADING. IF NOT, REWIND TAPE AND START LOADING PROCEDURE OVER.

PLAY
AS SOON AS IT LOADS ALL THE SCREEN WILL CLEAR AND THEN AGAIN SHOWING A MAZE. WHEN THE MAZE IS COMPLETED IT WILL PUT A DOOR SOMEWHERE ALONG EITHER THE TOP OF BOTTOM ROW OF MAZE. AFTER A FEW MOMENTS IT WILL SHOW WHERE YOU ARE IN THE MAZE. YOU MAY NOW EITHER SIT AND PAUSE FOR A FEW SECONDS TO PLAN YOUR STRATEGY OR JUST START. THE KEYS CELL THEN CHANGE FROM THE COMMAND KEY TO A GROUND LEVEL VIEW. YOU WILL HAVE TO USE THE MAZE IN WAY OF THE DOOR. YOU USE ONE KEY COMMAND WHICH WILL BRING UP A "PLAN VIEW" SO YOU CAN SEE WHERE THE ARROW AND EXIT IS IN THE MAZE. YOU CAN USE THIS WHENEVER YOU'RE FACING IN EITHER A NORTH, SOUTH, EAST, OR WEST DIRECTION IN A MAZE. IF THE ARROW IS FACING NORTH IF YOU WANT IT TO BE FACING SOUTH AND PROPER WORD WOULD BE SOUTH TO GET IT DOWN IN THE DOORWAY. THEN EAST AND WEST ARE SIMILAR. IF YOU FIND THE DOORWAY IT MAY BE A BIT CONFUSING AT FIRST, BUT IT IS WORTH THE EFFORT. AND UNTIL YOU CAN PRESS "Q" FOR QUIT, AND IT WILL SHOW YOU AN ESTIMATION OF THE MAZE. YOU TO DEVELOP A FEW MOMENTS TO APPEAR A KEY EXIT. THEN IT RETURNS TO THE MAGIC LEVEL SO YOU CAN REFINE YOUR BACKWARD. GAME OVER WHEN YOU ARE FREE OF THE MAZE. PRESS "ENTER" KEY TO PLAY AGAIN, GOOD LUCK......

NUFEKOP PRESENTS

DODGE CARS

THERE YOU ARE, JUST TAKING A NICE SUNDAY DRIVE DOWN THE FREEWAY, WHEN OUT OF NOWHERE THERE ARE CARS, HUNDREDS OF CARS, AND THEY'RE ALL HEADED STRAIGHT FOR YOU. YOU CAN DO YOUR BEST TO DODGE THEM, BUT IT'S DOUBTFUL YOU'LL SURVIVE.

REQUIRED
5K COMMODORE VIC 20 COMPUTER
COMMODORE TAPE PLAYER

LOADING
TURN COMPUTER ON, INSERT TAPE INTO PLAYER AND REWIND. PRESS AND HOLD DOWN THE SHIFT KEY THEN PRESS AND RELEASE THE RUN/STOP KEY. NOW RELEASE THE SHIFT KEY AND PRESS "PLAY" ON TAPE. AFTER A FEW MOMENTS THE SCREEN SHOULD SAY LOADING. IF NOT, REWIND TAPE AND START LOADING PROCEDURE OVER.

PLAY
THE OBJECT OF THE GAME IS TO AVOID THE ONCOMING TRAFFIC. USE LEFT AND RIGHT OF THE STICK TO CONTROL THE CAR. YOUR SCORE IS BASED ON HOW FAR DOWN THE FREEWAY THAT YOU GET. WHEN YOU CRASH, YOUR SCORE IS DISPLAYED IN THE UPPER LEFT OF THE SCREEN, FOLLOWED BY A DISPLAY OF THE TOP FIVE SCORES, AND FINALLY, SHOWN ON THE RIGHT HAND SIDE OF THE SCREEN, IS HOW YOU RATE OUT OF ALL THE PEOPLE WHO HAVE PLAYED. TO PLAY AGAIN PRESS THE FIRE BUTTON.

NUFEKOP PRESENTS

RACEWAY

RACEWAY IS A CAR RACE GAME FOR ONE OR TWO PLAYERS. WITH ONE PLAYER, YOU CAN RACE AGAINST THE ON THE TRACK, OR... LEGAL COURSE OUT TO TYPICALLY PICK UP KEYS TWO PLAYERS GOING AT EACH SET. EVEN WITH ACTIONS GET HARDER IN EACH PERSONS MIND. HAPPY RACING!

REQUIRED
5K COMMODORE VIC 20 COMPUTER
COMMODORE TAPE PLAYER

LOADING
TURN COMPUTER ON, INSERT TAPE INTO PLAYER AND REWIND. PRESS AND HOLD DOWN THE SHIFT KEY THEN PRESS AND RELEASE THE RUN/STOP KEY. NOW RELEASE THE SHIFT KEY AND PRESS "PLAY" ON TAPE. AFTER A FEW MOMENTS THE SCREEN SHOULD SAY LOADING. IF NOT, REWIND TAPE AND START LOADING PROCEDURE OVER.

OPTIONS
WHEN THE GAME IS LOADED IN, YOU WILL SEE THE PROMPT "NO. OF LAPS (1-99)?". YOU SHOULD NOW ENTER A NUMBER BETWEEN ONE AND TWENTY. TO START THE ACTION YOU... THE LONGER WILL TAKE UP TO 100 SPANNED OF THE RACETRACK THAT'S GREATER A CHANCE OF RACING ON. WHEN THE GAME IS OVER IT'S TO THE TRACK YOU WANT TO RACE ON. HIT THE SPACE BAR.

PLAY
THE CAR ON THE LEFT (PURPLE) USES "3G KEYS" Z AND "C" FOR RIGHT AND "B" (SPEED). THE CAR ON THE RIGHT (BLUE) USES THE SHIFT "*", "SHIFT, =" (RIGHT) AND "CRSR DOWN" FOR SPEED. YOU CAN TOO LEFT AND RIGHT OF THE CAR, AS IF YOU REMEMBER THE CAR. ALSO, YOU CANNOT TURN WHILE IT'S SPEED BUTTON IS PRESSED... SO JUST LET THE TRACK FOR A FEW INSTANCES. THE GAME WITH SPEED ALONE AND CAN ONLY BE PRESSED DOWN IT NORMAL SPEED OF A LAP. TO RESTART AGAIN, PRESS THE SPACE BAR.

37

nufekop PRESENTS

INVASION

YOU BETTER BE PREPARED FOR THE INVADER, BECAUSE HE ISN'T ABOUT TO GIVE YOU A CHANCE. TO STOP THE INVASION YOU MUST USE YOUR THRUST ROCKETS AND DROP BOMBS TO THEIR FULLEST POTENTIAL. YOU ARE IN CHARGE. GOOD LUCK.

REQUIRED
5K COMMODORE VIC 20 COMPUTER
COMMODORE TAPE PLAYER

LOADING
TURN COMPUTER ON, INSERT TAPE INTO PLAYER AND REWIND. PRESS AND HOLD DOWN THE SHIFT KEY THEN PRESS AND RELEASE THE RUN/STOP KEY. NOW RELEASE THE SHIFT KEY AND PRESS "PLAY" ON TAPE. AFTER A FEW MOMENTS THE SCREEN SHOULD SAY LOADING. IF NOT, REWIND TAPE AND START LOADING PROCEDURE OVER.

PLAY
AFTER THE GAME LOADS IN, THE PLAYFIELD WILL APPEAR AND THE GAME BEGINS. TO RELEASE THE DROP BOMBS, AND TO FIRE THE THRUST ROCKETS USE THE UP AND DOWN POSITIONS OF THE JOYSTICK. THE OBJECT OF THE GAME IS TO PROTECT THE FLASHING BLUE ENERGY PODS AT THE RIGHT OF THE SCREEN FOR AS LONG AS YOU CAN USING BOMBS AND ROCKETS. THE DARK BLUE ALIEN SHIP WILL COME IN FROM THE LEFT AND TRY TO MAKE IT PAST YOUR WEAPONRY AND GET THE ENERGY PODS. THE BOMBS (TOP OF SCREEN) FIRE ONE AT A TIME FROM LEFT TO RIGHT, AND THE ROCKETS (BOTTOM OF SCREEN) FIRE FROM RIGHT TO LEFT. IF YOU USE UP ALL YOUR ROCKETS AND BOMBS YOU WILL GET A NEW SET. ALSO, IF YOU HIT AN ALIEN SHIP AFTER HE HAS TAKEN ONE OF YOUR ENERGY PODS, YOU WILL GET THE POD BACK. THE GAME ENDS WHEN THE ALIEN ESCAPES WITH ALL FOUR PODS. INVASION SCORES AS FOLLOWS: 20 POINTS FOR INCOMING ALIENS (DARK BLUE), AND 10 POINTS FOR FLEEING ALIENS (LIGHT BLUE). AFTER PLAY IS OVER THE SCREEN WILL DISPLAY
SCORE. ANYTIME AFTER THE SCREEN DISPLAYS
A NEW GAME.

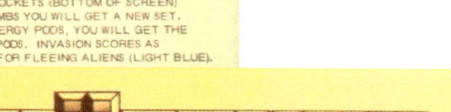

---

nufekop PRESENTS

KRAZY KONG

THE KRAZY GORILLA HAS TAKEN THREE FAIR MAIDENS UP TO THE TOP OF THE GIANT STAIRWAY AND YOU (BEING THE VALIANT HERO THAT YOU ARE) WILL ATTEMPT TO RESCUE THEM AT THE RISK OF YOUR OWN LIFE. GOOD LUCK!

REQUIRED
5K COMMODORE VIC 20 COMPUTER
COMMODORE TAPE PLAYER

LOADING
TURN COMPUTER ON, INSERT TAPE INTO PLAYER AND REWIND. PRESS AND HOLD DOWN THE SHIFT KEY THEN PRESS AND RELEASE THE RUN/STOP KEY. NOW RELEASE THE SHIFT KEY AND PRESS "PLAY" ON TAPE. AFTER A FEW MOMENTS THE SCREEN SHOULD SAY LOADING. IF NOT, REWIND TAPE AND START LOADING PROCEDURE OVER.

OPTIONS
F1: FEWER BARRELS AND LONGER JUMP
F3: FEWER BARRELS AND SHORT JUMP
F5: MORE BARRELS AND LONG JUMP
F7: MORE BARRELS AND SHORT JUMP

PLAY
THE OBJECT OF THE GAME IS TO JUMP UP THE STEPS AND GET TO THE FALLING MAIDENS AND SET TO THE MADDING LIGHT BLUE F SQUARE AT THE TOP OF THE SCREEN BEFORE YOU ARE OUT OF ENERGY. THE CONTROLS ARE AS F7 FOR LEFT TO GO RIGHT, AND F1 FOR JUMP OR USE THE LEFT & RIGHT OF JOYSTICK, AND THE ACTION BUTTON TO JUMP. DOWN THERE IS ALSO A BONUS SQUARE ONLY LIT UP FOR A SHORT TIME, YOU GET 100 POINTS IF YOU CAN MAKE IT TO IT IN TIME LIT UP. HAS A BARREL COMES DOWN YOU CAN JUMP OVER IT ONLY IF YOUR ENERGY SQUARE LIGHT UP RIGHT THEN IS OF JUMPING. YOU MUST JUMP BEFORE THE BARREL GETS TO YOU, BECAUSE YOU HAVE TO BE IN THE AIR IN ORDER TO GET A BARREL. YOU JUDGEMENT TOO. IF YOU DON'T YOU'LL BE KNOCKED. YOU WILL BE KILLED IF A BARREL HITS YOU WITHOUT YOUR JUMPING OR IF YOU DO A JUMP TOO CLOSE. IT'S EASY IF YOU JUMP BEFORE SHE GETS. ALSO WHEN YOU REACH A SMALL MAIDEN FORMCELL GAME ENDS WHEN YOU ARE KILLED OR OUT OF ENERGY OR HAVE RESCUED ALL THREE MAIDEN.
QUICKLY PRESS SPACE BAR TO PLAY AGAIN, AS IF TWO RUNS STARTS IT MAY PLAY IT'S ENTIRETY.

---

nufekop PRESENTS

QUIRK

HERE'S A FAST PACED GAME THAT'LL KEEP YOU HOPPING BACK FOR MORE. AS YOU WORK YOUR WAY UP AND DOWN THE LEVELS CATCHING THE FALLING OBJECTS, YOU ARE CONSTANTLY AWARE THAT ONE MISTAKE AND YOU COULD FALL DOWN INTO THE DEADLY SPIKES! GOOD LUCK.

REQUIRED
5K COMMODORE VIC 20 COMPUTER
COMMODORE TAPE PLAYER

LOADING
TURN COMPUTER ON, INSERT TAPE INTO PLAYER AND REWIND. PRESS AND HOLD DOWN THE SHIFT KEY THEN PRESS AND RELEASE THE RUN/STOP KEY. NOW RELEASE THE SHIFT KEY AND PRESS "PLAY" ON TAPE. AFTER A FEW MOMENTS THE SCREEN SHOULD SAY LOADING. IF NOT, REWIND TAPE AND START LOADING PROCEDURE OVER.

PLAY
THE OBJECT OF THE GAME IS TO SCORE AS MANY POINTS AS IS POSSIBLE BY CATCHING THE FALLING SAD FACES. YOU CONTROL THE PLAYER BY USING LEFT AND RIGHT OF STICK TO MOVE FIGURE, AND THE ACTION BUTTON ON STICK FOR JUMP. YOU CAN MOVE FROM LEVEL TO LEVEL BY EITHER JUMPING OR FALLING THROUGH THE HOLES IN THE MOVING FLOORS. EVERY SAD FACE YOU HIT IS WORTH 10 POINTS. IF YOU CAN WORK YOUR WAY TO THE TOP LEVEL, YOU CAN JUMP UP AND HIT THE LIGHT BLUE POWER PODS THAT MAKE THE NEXT SAD FACE YOU HIT WORTH 40 POINTS. GAME ENDS WHEN YOU FALL DOWN INTO THE SPIKES AT THE BOTTOM OF SCREEN THREE TIMES, OR WHEN FIVE SAD FACES MAKE IT TO THE SPIKES. ALSO, WHEN YOUR SCORE GOES OVER 300 THE HOLES IN THE FLOORS DOUBLE THEIR SIZE, INCREASING DIFFICULTY.
HIT SPACE BAR TO START A NEW GAME.

---

nufekop PRESENTS

JOURNEY

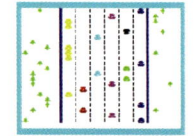

YOU'RE ON A JOURNEY INTO THE DEPTHS OF A CAVERN THAT JETS RICH WITH INTERCALCULATED EMBS. SO ENTER IF YOU ARE CALCULATED THAT THERE SHOULD BE SOME CAVERNS WITHIN THE CAVE TO TRY TO KEEP POWER ALIVE. IT'S ALL UP TO THE PILOT NOW. GOOD LUCK!

REQUIRED
5K COMMODORE VIC 20 COMPUTER
COMMODORE TAPE PLAYER

LOADING
TURN COMPUTER ON, INSERT TAPE INTO PLAYER AND REWIND. PRESS AND HOLD DOWN THE SHIFT KEY THEN PRESS AND RELEASE THE RUN/STOP KEY. NOW RELEASE THE SHIFT KEY AND PRESS "PLAY" ON TAPE. AFTER A FEW MOMENTS THE SCREEN SHOULD SAY LOADING. IF NOT, REWIND TAPE AND START LOADING PROCEDURE OVER.

PLAY
THE OBJECT OF THE GAME IS TO GET AS FAR DOWN INTO THE CAVERN AS YOU CAN. YOU MUST AVOID YOUR FUEL, AND WE CAN SHOOT UP OF FUEL, YOU MAY SCROLL UP A LONG LEFT SIDE. THE CONTROLS ARE DIAGRAMMED FOR RIGHT TO THE JOYSTICK. YES, BOTTOM FOR LEFT STICK TO GO. YOU HAVE TO CONCENTRATE ON LEFT ARE RIGHT. SOME ADDITIONAL FUEL. JUST JUMP INTO THE OBJECTS MARKED "FUEL". THE GAME ENDS WHEN YOU CRASH INTO ANYTHING. YOUR SCORE IS BASED ON HOW FAR DOWN THE CAVERN YOU GOT A IT.
HIT THE SPACE BAR TO PLAY AGAIN.

HUSKUP PRESENTS

P.O. BOX 156   SHADY COVE, OR 97539

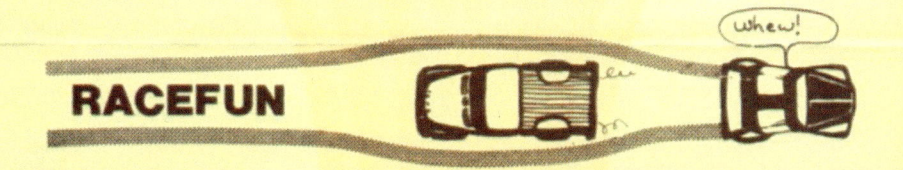

RACEFUN

whew!

REQUIRED
STANDARD 5K VIC 20 COMPUTER
VIC 1530 DATASSETTE

LOADING
TURN COMPUTER ON, INSERT TAPE AND REWIND. PRESS AND HOLD (SHIFT), THEN PRESS AND RELEASE (RUN/STOP) AND RELEASE (SHIFT). PRESS (PLAY) ON THE TAPE PLAYER. AFTER A MOMENT THE SCREEN WILL SAY "LOADING". IF NOT, REPEAT LOADING PROCEDURE.

PLAY
USE FORWARD ON THE JOYSTICK OR THE (F1) KEY ON YOUR VIC FOR THE THROTTLE, BACK ON THE STICK OR (F7) FOR BRAKES RIGHT OR LEFT OF STICK OR (Z) AND (C) KEYS FOR LEFT AND RIGHT STEERING.

POINTS ARE BASED ON A SLIDING SCALE OF DISTANCE * SPEED. FOR EXAMPLE, IF YOU PASS 100 CARS AT MAX THROTTLE YOUR SCORE WILL BE MUCH HIGHER THAN IF YOU PASSED THEM AT MINIMUM SPEED.

PRESS SPACE BAR OR USE FIRE BUTTON TO PLAY AGAIN.

DRIVE CAREFULLY.

These instructions generally told you if the game needed a joystick, paddle or extended memory cartridge, how to load the game and get it running, and finally a brief overview of how to play it.

P.O. BOX 156 — **NUFEKOP** — SHADY COVE, OR 97539

PRESENTS

SPACE QUEST

FAR, FAR AWAY FROM NOW, IN A TIME WHEN MANS KNOWLEDGE OF SPACE AND TIME HAS RECENTLY REDUCED THE VASTNESS OF OUR ENTIRE GALAXY INTO A MAPPED SERIES OF ACCESSABLE QUADRANTS. EVEN IN THESE MOST GLORIOUS OF TIMES A DARKNESS HAS CREPT IN AND IS THREATENING TO EXTINGUISH THE BRIGHT BURNING LIGHT OF FREEDOM.

NOW AS ALL WATCHERS ARE AWARE, PEACE AND FREEDOM ARE SYNONYMOUS WITH GROWTH AND EXPANSION, THE VERY THINGS BEING THREATENED BY THIS HORROR, THE BLIGHT OF THE MICROCHINES. IRONY, A FACTOR IN MOST FUTURE SHAPING EQUASIONS, HAS CERTAINLY NOT NEGLECTED THIS ONE. SOME 2000 YEARS PAST, THINKING TO PUT AN END TO WAR, ALL INTELLIGENT ROBOT CONTROLLED BATTLE CRAFT AND OTHER WAR WAGING MACHINERY WERE DEPOSITED ON A BARREN, AIRLESS ASTROID AND SENT ON A ONE WAY TRIP INTO DEEP SPACE. THESE GHOSTS OF WAR HAVE RETURNED TO HAUNT THEIR CREATORS. AS MANKINDS PERIMETERS EXPANDED THEY FOUND WAITING AMONG THE STARS, ROBOTS MORE ADVANCED THAN ANY THEY HAD CAST OUT THOSE TEN CENTURIES EARLIER. THESE MACHINES HAVE NOT ONLY REPAIRED, BUT IMPROVED THEMSELVES, AND NEW DEVELOPMENTS HAVE CHANGED THIS RELATIVELY ISOLATED PROBLEM INTO ONE WITH FAR REACHING, FUTURE CHANGING IMPLICATIONS. GALAXY CENTRAL, THE MASSIVE COMPUTER USED BY ALL JUMP SHIPS TO GUIDE THEM INTO SAFE HYPER-SPACE LINES, HAS REPORTED SOME DEVASTATING EVENTS. MICROCHINE FIGHTERS HAVE RECENTLY JUMPED INTO SCATTERED QUADRANTS ALL OVER THE GALAXY AND THE LAST THREE EXPLORATION SHIPS TO HAVE GRAND CENTRAL PLOT THEIR JUMPS RECEIVED TAMPERED WITH DATA AND ENDED THEIR LEAPS IN TWO SUNS AND ONE PREVIOUSLY VERY LARGE PLANET. NEED WE TELL YOU THE DANGERS OF THESE HEARTLESS KILLING MACHINES NOW THAT THEY HAVE STOLEN THE SECRETS OF HYPER-SPACE AND HAVE RENDERED OUR OWN JUMPSHIPS VIRTUALLY USELESS BECAUSE OF THE TAMPERING.

ONE SHIP, "SKYE'S LIMITED II", HAS BEEN EQUIPPED, LIKE ITS NAME ORIGINATING PREDECESSOR FROM THE DISTANT PAST, WITH EVERY FEATURE CURRENTLY AVAILABLE INCLUDING THE ABILITY TO, USING THE GALAXY MAP, PLOT AND JUMP INDEPENDANT OF G. CENTRAL.

WE KNOW THE MICROCHINES HAVE SPENT MANY OF THEIR NUMBER IN THEIR EFFORT TO UNRAVEL TIME/SPACE FABRIC AND ARE CURRENTLY, ACCORDING TO THE ANALYSTS, VULNERABLE TO THE ATTACK OF A ONE MAN FIGHTER LIKE "SKYE'S". THEY, AS A FOOTNOTE, MENTION THAT GIVEN JUST A LITTLE TIME TO REPRODUCE THEMSELVES, THE MICROCHINES WILL ESTABLISH A FOOTHOLD IN THE GALAXY THAT WOULD BE NEARLY UNBREAKABLE.

SO MY FRIEND AND HUMANKINDS ONLY HOPE, MAY YOUR HAND BE STEADY AND YOUR MIND BE CLEAR, FOR UNLESS YOU RETURN VICTORIOUS WE, THE CHILDREN OF THE STARS, FACE A CERTAINLY HORRIBLE AND POSSIBLY SHORT, FUTURE.

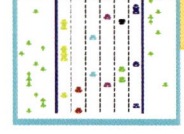

SPACE QUEST

REQUIRED
VIC20 COMPUTER
VIC 1530 DATASSETTE
8K MEMORY EXPANDER

LOADING
INSTALL MEMORY EXPANDER AND TURN ON COMPUTER. INSERT AND REWIND "SPACE QUEST". PRESS AND HOLD THE LEFT HAND (SHIFT) KEY, THEN PRESS AND RELEASE THE (RUN/STOP) KEY FOLLOWING WITH THE RELEASE OF (SHIFT). NOW YOU HAVE ONLY TO PRESS (PLAY) ON THE DATASSETTE TO COMPLETE THE HUMAN PART OF THE PROCEDURES. ON A LOAD ERROR ERROR, REAPEAT ENTIRE PROCEDURE. HINT: DATASSETTE SHOULD BE AS FAR AS POSSIBLE (AT LEAST 3 FT.) FROM TV OR MONITOR.

PLAY
"SPACE QUEST" IS ACTUALLY A SIMULATED DAY IN THE LIFE OF A SPACE HERO. AFTER LOADING YOU WILL BE CONFRONTED WITH YOUR FIRST DECISION, WHICH LEVEL OF HEROING ARE YOU UP TO? YOUR CHOICES ARE: (F1) BEGINNER, (F3) NOVICE, (F5) INTERMEDIATE, (F7) EXPERT.
AFTER DECIDING AND PRESSING THE APPROPRIATE FUNCTION KEY, YOU WILL BE TRANSFERRED AUTOMATICALLY TO THE "GALAXY MAP".

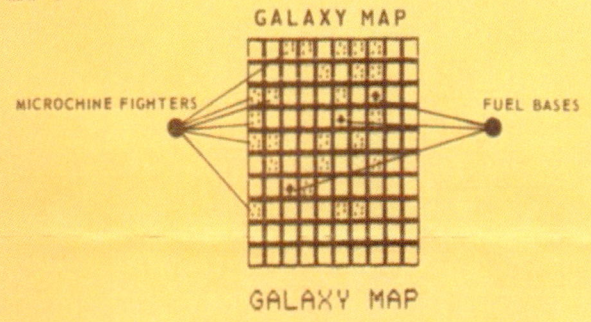

GALAXY MAP

MICROCHINE FIGHTERS — FUEL BASES

GALAXY MAP

FUEL:

THIS MAP IS USED TO DETERMINE YOUR NEXT HYPER-SPACE JUMP DESTINATION. BY MOVING THE FLASHING SQUARE TO THE QUADRANT YOU WISH TO JUMP INTO AND PRESSING H (for hyper-space) A CONTROLLED TEAR WILL APPEAR IN THE FABRIC OF THE UNIVERSE AND YOU WILL SLIP THROUGH AND LAND IN THE QUADRANT CHOSEN.

WARNING: AS YOUR JUMPS ARE BEING PROCESSED THROUGH "SKYES LIMITED'S" "VIC" LINE COMPUTERS INSTEAD OF THE MAMMOTH SYSTEMS AT GALAXY CENTRAL THERE IS NO GUARANTEE YOU WILL NOT COME OUT OF HYPER-SPACE AND FIND YOURSELF IN THE MIDDLE OF AN ASTROID FIELD. IF THIS HAPPENS, THE NORMALLY FRONTAL VIEW RADAR WILL AUTOMATICALLY SWITCH TO VERTICAL. YOUR SHIP AND THE ASTROIDS THAT YOU ARE ABOUT TO RUN INTO WILL BE SHOWN FROM AN OVERHEAD VIEW. USING LEFT AND RIGHT ON THE STICK YOU MUST DODGE THESE ASTROIDS UNTIL CLEAR SPACE IS SHOWN ON THE SCREEN. YOUR RADAR SWITCHES BACK AUTOMATICALLY TO A FORWARD VIEW.

NOW, YOU SHOULD FIND YOURSELF CONFRONTED WITH ONE OF THREE POSSIBILITIES. IF YOU CHOOSE TO CONFRONT THE ENEMY AND JUMPED INTO AN INFECTED AREA, THE DOG FIGHT IS GOING TO BEGIN. THE MICROCHEEN ATTACK IS A SIMPLE ONE, THEY RUN IN GROUPS OF FOUR AND ONE AT A TIME THEY TRY TO COLLIDE INTO YOUR SHIP, SO QUICKLY AS YOU ARE ABLE, LINE THEM UP IN THE CROSSHAIRS, PRESS THE FIRE BUTTON AND WATCH FOR THE NEXT ONE. THE SECOND POSSIBILITY IS THAT YOUR JUMP WAS A FUEL STOP. AS THE FUEL CATCHES HAVE BEEN HIDDEN FROM THE MICROCHEENS DEEP INSIDE PLANETOIDS, EVEN FUELING UP HAS BECOME A CHALLENGE. AGAIN THE RADAR WILL SWITCH FROM FRONTAL TO AN OVERHEAD OR VERTICAL VIEW. THE FUEL WILL BE FOUND AT THE BOTTOM OF THE TREACHEROUS CAVER. AFTER SUCCESSFULLY NEGOTIATING THE CAVERN AND FUELING UP, THE GALAXY MAP WILL AUTOMATICALLY COME UP BECAUSE YOU MUST JUMP OUT OF THESE PLANETOIDS THEREBY DESTROYING IT TO PREVENT ANALIZATION OR USE BY THE ENEMY. THE THIRD POSSIBILITY IS THAT BY HURRYING TOO MUCH AT THE GALAXY MAP YOU ACCIDENTALLY JUMPED INTO AN EMPTY QUADRANT. IF THIS HAS HAPPENED, UNLESS YOU COME OUT IN AN ASTROID FIELD, NOTHING WILL HAPPEN. YOU MUST PRESS G, CALLING UP THE GALAXY MAP AND PLOT A NEW JUMP.

The quality of the printing was subject to change on every game.

Every time we were at the printers we'd have them print a few hundred of some game, but we'd always be out of one we needed, so in a pinch we'd just photocopy them to get some product out the door.

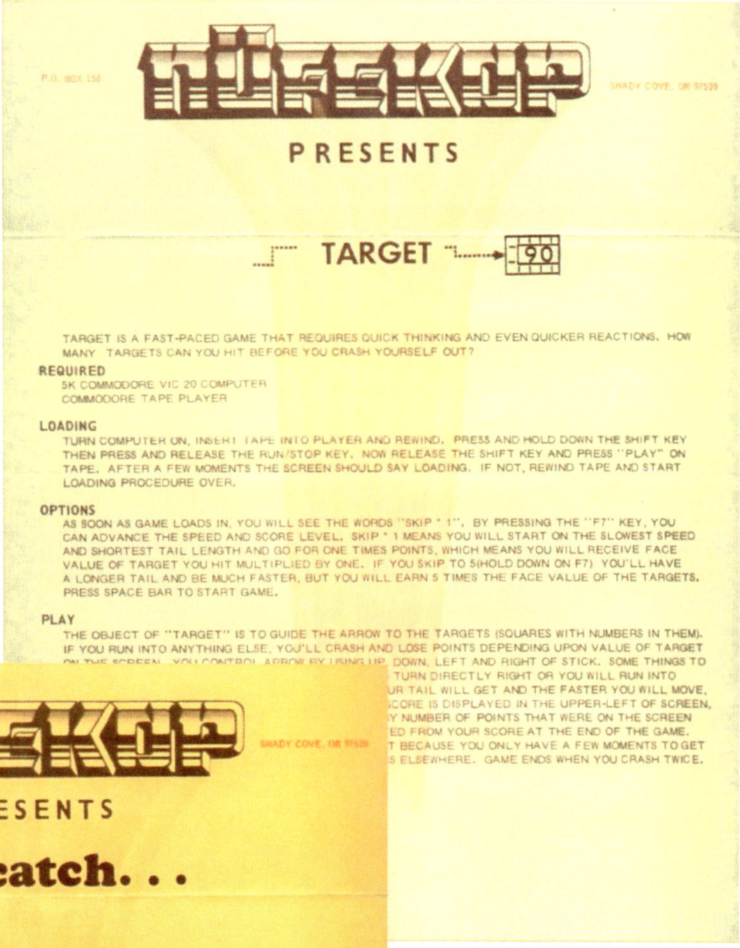

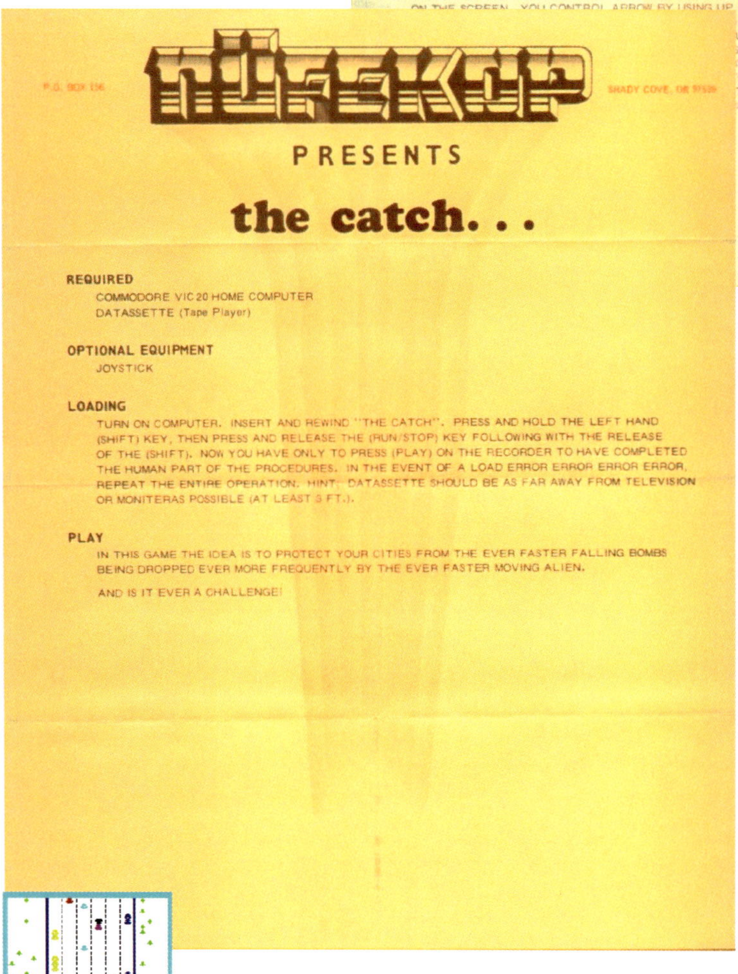

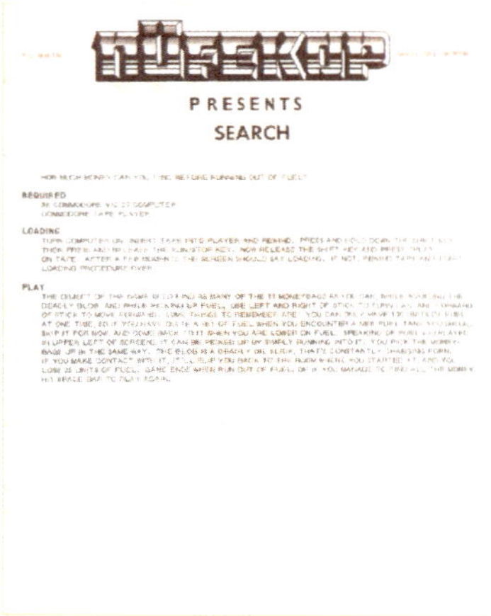

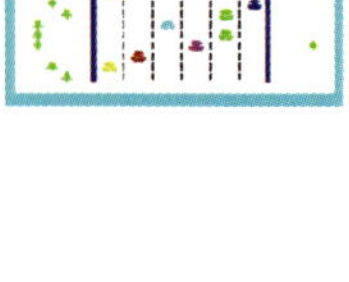

NUFEKOP PRESENTS

VIKMAN

P.O. BOX 156   SHADY COVE, OR 97539

DON'T STOP NOW, YOU'VE GOT THREE MONSTERS RIGHT ON YOUR TRAIL. ALL YOU NEED TO DO IS EAT A FEW MORE DOTS AND YOU'LL COMPLETE YOUR FIRST MISSION. THE MONSTERS ARE CLOSING IN ON YOU. GOOD LUCK!!

REQUIRED
5K COMMODORE VIC 20 COMPUTER
COMMODORE TAPE PLAYER

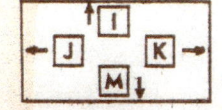

LOADING
TURN COMPUTER ON, INSERT TAPE INTO PLAYER AND REWIND. VIKMAN IS RECORDED WITH THE KEYBOARD VERSION FOLLOWING THE JOYSTICK VERSION ON BOTH SIDES OF TAPE. TO USE KEYBOARD SET THE FOOT COUNTER TO ZERO AND FAST FORWARD THE TAPE UNTIL IT REACHES 40. PRESS AND HOLD DOWN THE SHIFT KEY THEN PRESS AND RELEASE THE RUN/STOP KEY. NOW RELEASE THE SHIFT KEY AND PRESS "PLAY" ON TAPE. AFTER A FEW SECONDS THE SCREEN SHOULD SAY LOADING. IF NOT, REWIND TAPE AND START LOADING PROCEDURE OVER.

OPTIONS
AS SOON AS THE GAME LOADS IN, IT WILL ASK "HOW MANY MONSTERS (1-3)?". IF YOU TYPE '1' (RETURN), YOU WILL ONLY HAVE ONE MONSTER TO DEAL WITH BUT HE WILL MOVE EXACTLY THE SAME SPEED AS YOU. WITH 2 OR 3 MONSTERS YOU WILL HAVE A SPEED ADVANTAGE OVER THEM BUT YOU WILL HAVE MORE TO CONTEND WITH SO TRY THEM ALL AND FIND WHICH ONE SUITS YOUR SKILL AND TASTES.

PLAY
YOU CONTROL THE ROUND PLAYER AT THE TOP OF THE SCREEN USING THE KEYS PICTURED ABOVE. IF YOU HAVE JOYSTICK VERSION OF VIKMAN THEN YOU USE UP, DOWN, LEFT, AND RIGHT OF JOYSTICK TO MOVE PLAYER. THE OBJECT OF THE GAME IS TO CLEAR AWAY THE DOTS WITHOUT A MONSTER POUNCING ON YOU. YOU WILL RECEIVE BONUS LIVES AFTER CLEARING YOUR 2, 4, AND 6'TH SCREENS (IF YOU CAN MAKE IT THAT FAR). AFTER LOSING ALL OF YOUR LIVES (SHOWN IN THE UPPER RIGHT OF SCREEN) THE GAME DISPLAYS YOUR FINAL SCORE THEN ENDS. TO PLAY AGAIN, HIT THE SPACE BAR.

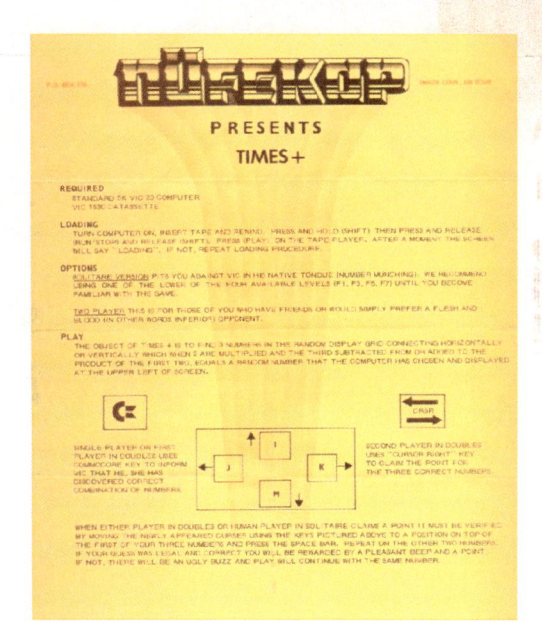

Advertisements.

We needed to run ads in magazines. Compute! And Compute's Gazette were the premiere place to put them. Ads cost between $300 and $3000 which was a fair amount of money back then, but it paid off.

This was our very first ad that ran in Compute! magazine. It was a quarter page black and white.

Not too fancy, but It introduced us and made sure that people knew we had the games available as this was when the word "vaporware" was invented.

A lot of companies ran ads at this same time but the product wouldn't ship, it was always "coming soon".

A few months later this half page ad was running in a few popular magazines.

Our catalog is now free instead of charging fifty cents for it.

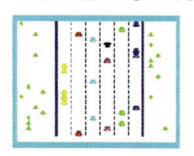

nüFEKOP FOR THE VIC-20

HARD SOFTWARE TO BEAT

ANY 5 $42.00 : ANY 3 $27.00 : ANY 1 $9.95 : OUR CATALOG FREE!

SEARCH – Drive through a giant maze of rooms encountering money bags, fuel tanks, and moving oil slicks that slide you back to start. Specify Keyboard or Joystick.

ALIEN PANIC – Climb ladders, dig holes and drop aliens . . . Quickly! Specify Keyboard or Joystick.

KRAZY KONG – You have to climb to the top but this crazy monkey keeps rolling barrels!?

VIKMAN – Sweep up dots before monsters mop you up.

RESCUE from NUFON – A Graphic Adventure game played with the keyboard. Some commands are; N.S.E.W. for direction, T for transport, U and D for the 5 floor elevator. Under your watchful eye (there are certain undesireables in these rooms) your guy finds and transports humans to safety. One player average 20 min.

INVASION – Protect energy pods from being stolen by enemy ships. Simple and challenging. Specify Keyboard or Joystick.

DEFENDER ON TRI $12.95 – Pilot a defender style ship through 4 screens worth of million year old alien machinery. Since this is probably your most common dream, we need say no more. No more . . . . . Requires 3K memory expander.

nüFROM DEPT.
Introducing 3D MAN – $12.95

Imagine for a moment the following: Take the maze from probably the most popular arcade game around, put it in the memory of your Vic 20, alter the perspective to eye level, put the dots back in, the monsters back in, the power dots to enable you to eat them, keep a running score, throw in cherrys and other symbols as rewards for clearing maze and some other special touches like a form of radar . . . . . its available from us Right Now! 3D MAN requires 3K expander.

WRITE nüFEKOP
P.O. BOX 156
SHADY COVE, OREGON 97539

FOREIGN ORDERS ADD ABOUT $1.50 PER TAPE

OR CALL 503-878-2113

MASTERCARD – VISA – C.O.D.

Here's our next couple ads. Gary, our ad-man, was trying to standardize a layout that made it easy to roll in a "Nufrom" featured product.

---

nüFEKOP FOR THE VIC-20

HARD SOFTWARE TO BEAT

ANY 5 $42.00 : ANY 3 $27.00 : ANY 1 $9.95 : OUR CATALOG FREE!

SEARCH – Drive through a giant maze of rooms encountering money bags, fuel tanks, and moving oil slicks that slide you back to start. Nobody here has ever gotten all eighteen bags–but we're still at it and soon . . .

ALIEN PANIC – Climb ladders, dig holes and drop aliens . . . Quickly!

KRAZY KONG – You have to climb to the top but this crazy monkey keeps rolling barrels!?

VIKMAN – Sweep up dots before monsters mop you up.

QUIRK – Arcade type game where if you're not awake the floor literally moves out from under your feet. Fortunately for the careful (and the Quick) the rewards roll into your pocket.

RESCUE from NUFON – A Graphic Adventure game played with the keyboard. Some commands are: N.S.E.W. for direction, T for transport, U and D for the 5 floor elevator. Under your watchful eye (there are certain undesireables in these rooms) your guy finds and transports humans to safety. One player average 20 min.

DODGE CARS – Fast fun on crowed freeway. This colorful game keeps top 5 & compares against last 50.

INVASION – Protect energy pods from being stolen by enemy ships. Simple and challenging.

******* SPECIFY KEYBOARD OR JOYSTICK *******

nüFROM DEPT.
EXTENDED MEMORY & DISK GAMES
AVAILABLE BY TIME OF PRINTING
WRITE FOR NEW CATALOG

Also 32K Krazy Kong for the ATARI

WRITE nüFEKOP
P.O. BOX 156
SHADY COVE, OREGON 97539

OR CALL 503-878-2113

MASTERCARD – VISA – C.O.D.

This was the first full page color ad from Nüfekop.

It offered just the best games, causing these titles to outsell all our others ten to one.

In December issues we ran these special "Merry Christmas" ads. These were among the first ones to offer our new innovation, the "Cassettalog".

46

This was one of our last full page color ads. It was also printed as a flyer and sent out to stores to hand out.

Resellers. This was a whole new world to us, but we quickly caught on to dealing with sales reps and wholesalers.

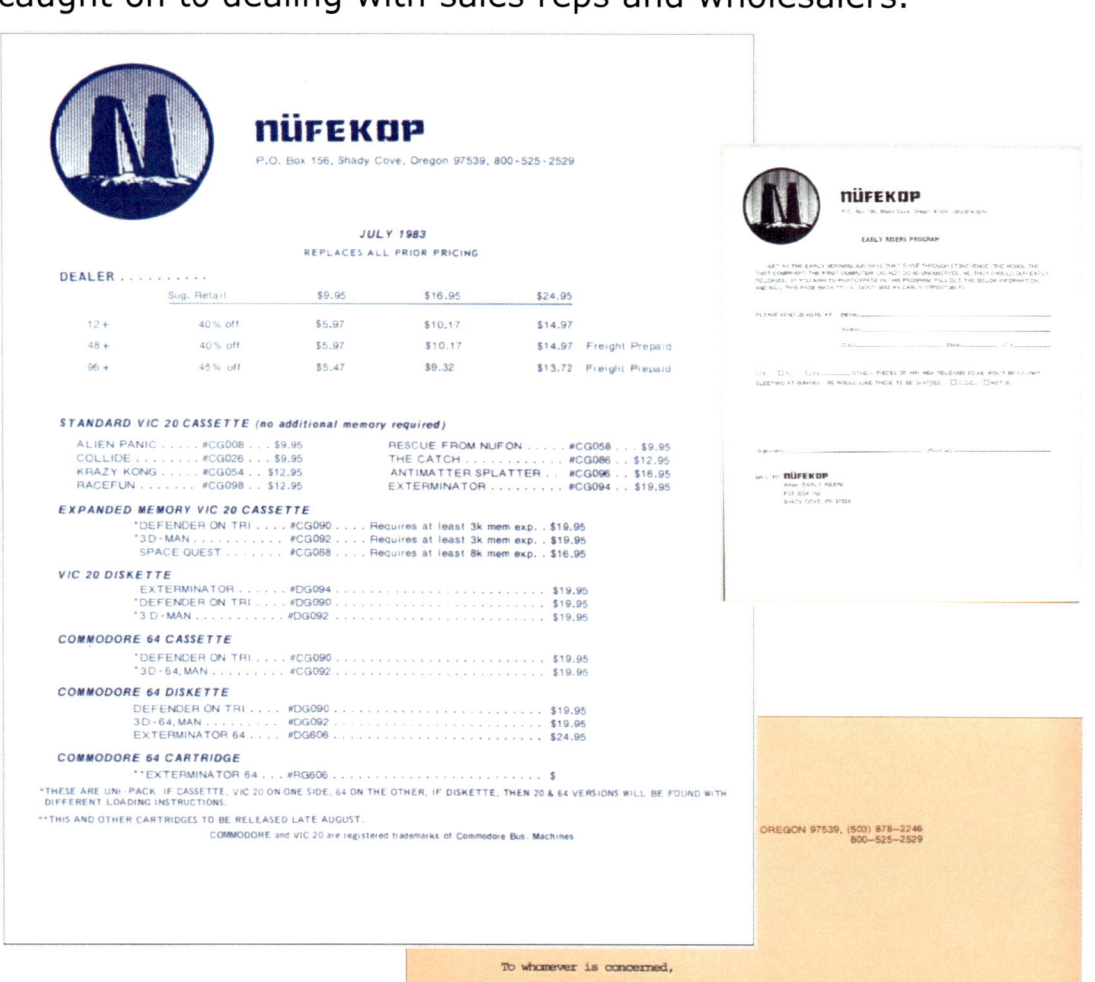

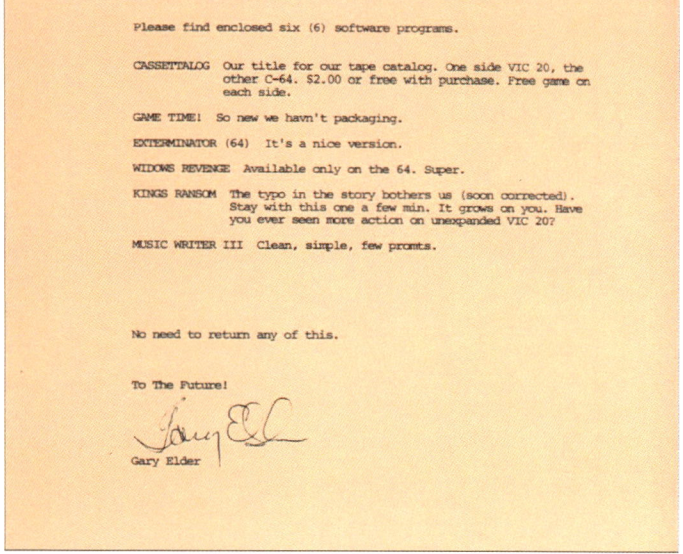

Here are some examples of letters that went to retailers and wholesalers that show pricing deals, return forms and bill collections in the form of a story.

NÜFEKOP

P.O. Box 156, Shady Cove, Oregon 97539, (503) 878-2246

Atten: Accounting Dept.

Re: Invoice number(s) _____

Read This,

A very old tale known quite well by the Druid Culture, though it took place many generations before Stonehenge, went something like this....

In the very young days of earth when the animals & birds knew not what they know now about themselves lived a small furry friendly animal called a lem. They existed mostly by eating seeds, nuts, and berries. They bred very efficiently, producing large litters. Unfortunately they were the primary food source for hawks, cats, wolves, and other preditors. Having no natural defenses they were unable to increase their number to even a comfortable level.

Now the leader of the lems understood the the preditors were dependant on the lems for food and did not spite them for it, as it is the way. All he wished for was just one passing of the moon without payment to the preditors. "This one short month would establish the lem population to where they would never have to worry again" he explained to the forests Eldest Oak. The Eldest Oak granted the lem the ability to hide and to blend into almost any forest setting, thus escaping the preditors. In return the lems would send forth at the end of each month enough of thier kind to feed the other forest animals.

The first month was wonderful. The lems played and mated and all lived. Joy abounded.

But the month past. The lem did not put forth the necessary payment. The preditory animals could not last much beyond 30 days without food. Some left, some died. The wise oak watched this all. He watched the last preditor leave the forest. He observed the daily increase in the lem population. He understood as nature sternly corrected this imbalance. You see the lems had brought a ghastly curse upon themselves, with no more natural selection, nature had to turn to other means. The indignity of it, the hopelessness, knowing that every so often your kind is victim to the whims of certain genetic codes and when the population gets just a little too heavy, those codes click and your driving force becomes self-destruction.

As the penalties for the breech of natures laws are often executed swiftly and decisively, so must some of mans laws. Not because anyone here likes to do it, but rather because of the delicate economical situation around us. It will not tolerate broken commitments and promises.

Please Respond to this last notice!

NÜFEKOP

P. O. BOX 156, SHADY COVE, OREGON 97539, (503) 878-2246
800-525-2529

Dear prior Distributer:

These samples are to bring you current on the new faces at NUFEKOP. Please remove the shrink film and find enclosed one of our newest hits.

If you have not ordered from our company recently, we hope this sample and the following offer will encourage you to renew our relationship.

NUFEKOP 1/2 GROSS PLAN
Choose a total of 5 dozen (60) pieces from the following Best Sellers list. These will be priced at 50% off retail.

VIC 20
EXTERMINATOR
MUSIC WRITER
KINGS RANSOM

CBM 64
EXTERMINATOR 64
KIDONS REVENGE

Now choose one more dozen to get 1/2 gross. They will be priced at 5¢. See how we are.

To the Future,
Gary Elder

NÜFEKOP

P.O. Box 156, Shady Cove, Oregon 97539, (503)878-2246

ACCOMPANY YOUR RETURNS WITH THIS FORM FOR CONVENIENCE AND ACCURACY.

Date _____
P.O. # _____

Company Name _____
Address _____
City _____ State _____ Zip _____

We are returning the following merchandise.

QUAN.	TITLE	QUAN.	TITLE
( )		( )	
( )		( )	
( )		( )	
( )		( )	
( )		( )	

Total Suggested Retail on the Above. $ _____ (use old higher prices)

We wish to receive in new packaging the following.

QUAN.	TITLE	QUAN.	TITLE
( )		( )	
( )		( )	
( )		( )	
( )		( )	
( )		( )	

Total Suggested Retail on the Above. $ _____ (use new lower prices)

Freight costs in returning this package. $ _____

There were three posters made that were sent to retailers featuring six of the better selling games.

50

A talented local artist did all the art and cut the color separations by hand rather than by photo process.

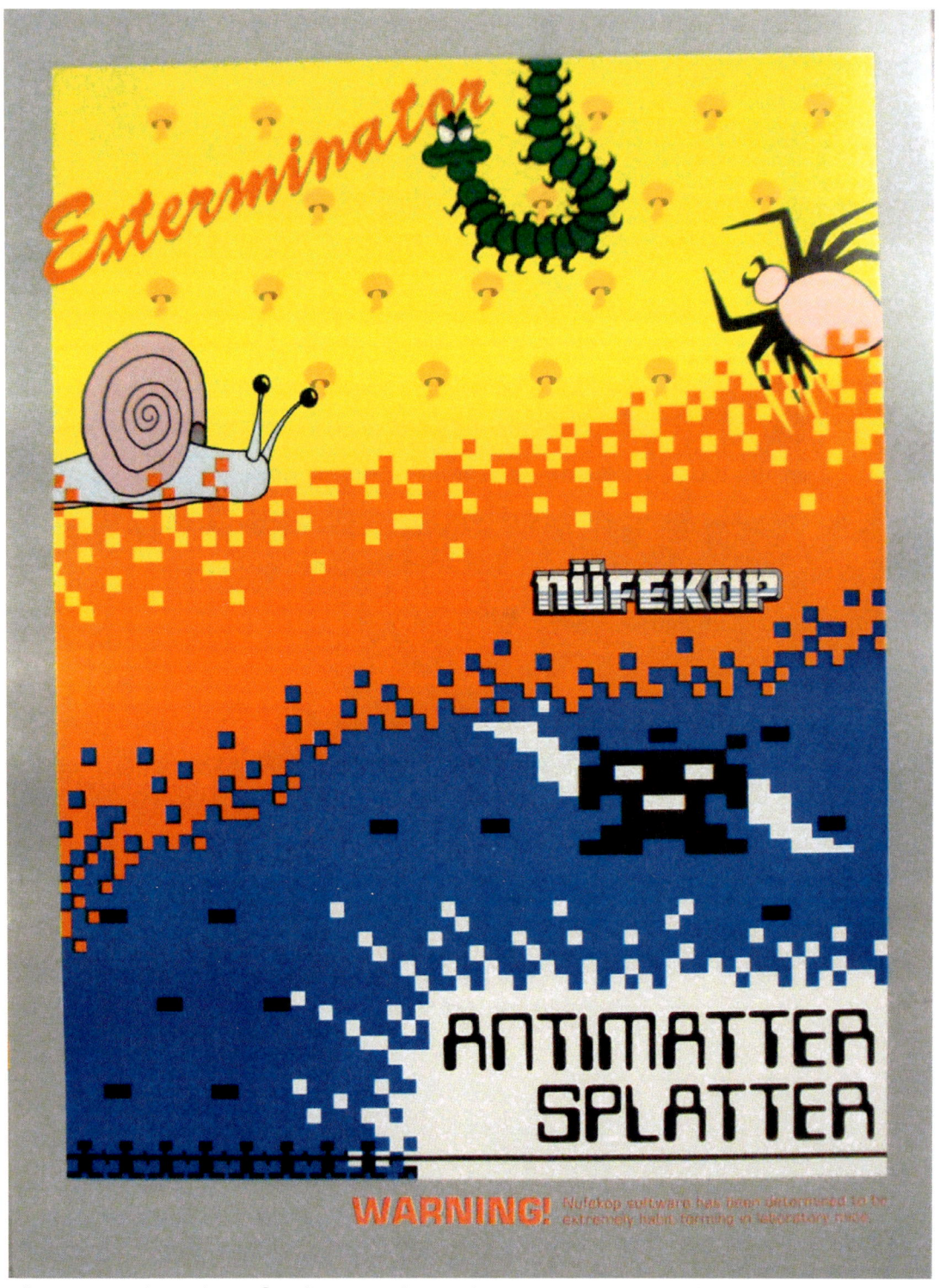

They are hard to find now, but they are some classic pieces.
I still have a set hanging in my living room.

52

The Cassette Tapes.
If you sell tapes, you need labels and we had a ton of them. They were all applied by hand. You'd label tapes till your vision went blurry, then move on to another job.

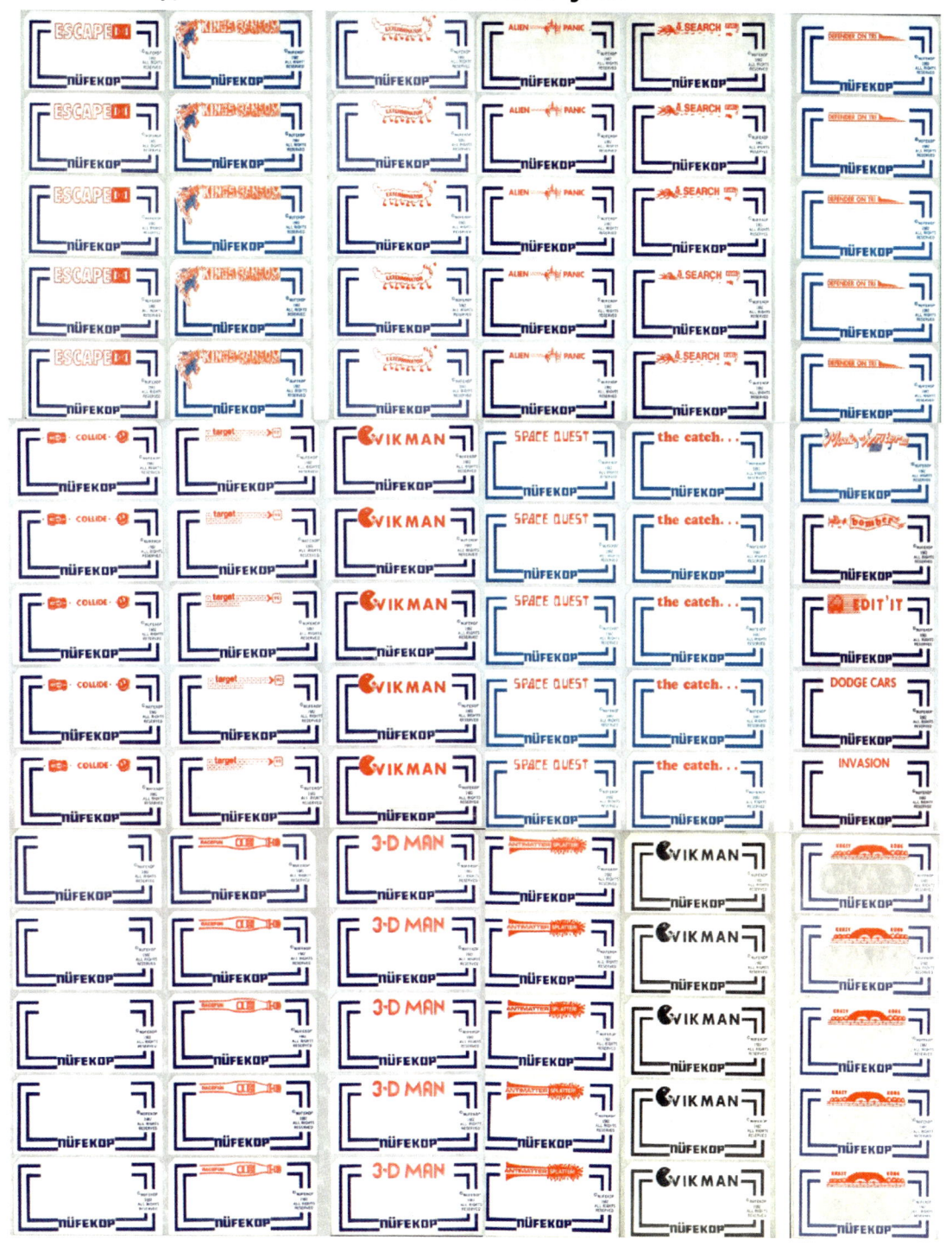

We saw this gold label paper, had a bunch of generic labels printed with the idea we'd use some sort of ink stamp to put the games name on them, but found out the inks would run and streak and never really dry up right.
Nearly a great idea.

```
**** CBM BASIC V2 ****
3583 BYTES FREE
READY.
LOAD
PRESS PLAY ON TAPE
```

This screen will be very familiar to all you old Vic users.

You'd type load and it would remind you to press play, which you'd do, only to eventually find out that you forgot to rewind first!

Around the office there was always stacks and stacks of tapes.

The standard clear tape cases were called "norelco's", named after the company that invented cassette tapes.

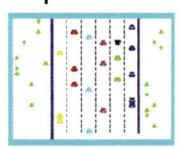

We did a lot of the tape duplicating ourselves, but we also used out-of-house help. These are masters sent for approval from a recording house in Colorado. Even though we had purchased a couple high-end tape duplicators, we could hardly keep up with demand.

The Fancy Packaging.
As the market got more sophisticated, so did our product.

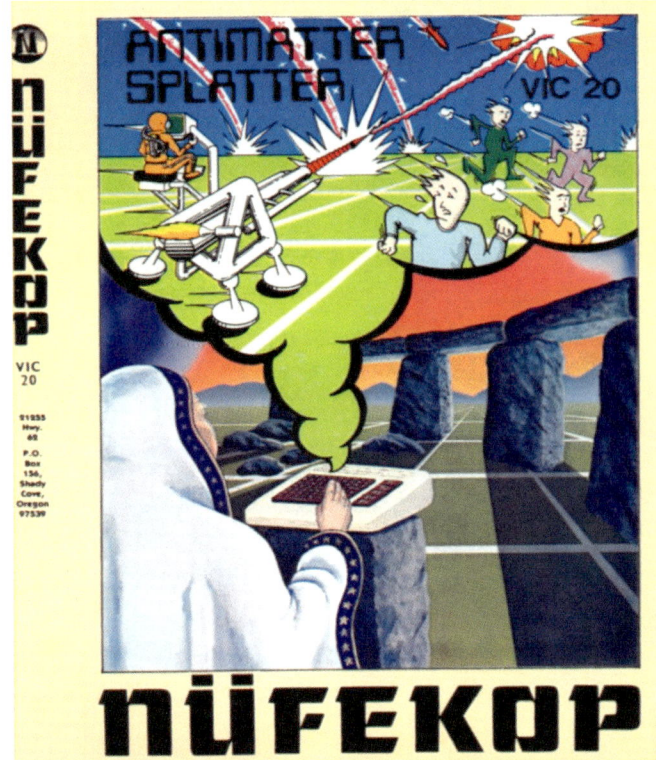

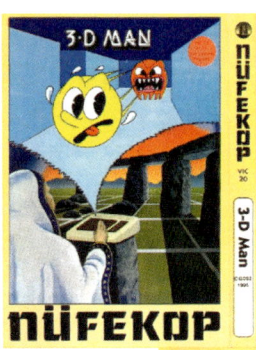

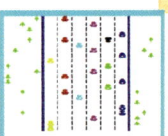

This is our line of boxes that could be used with cassette tapes or diskettes depending on the insert used.

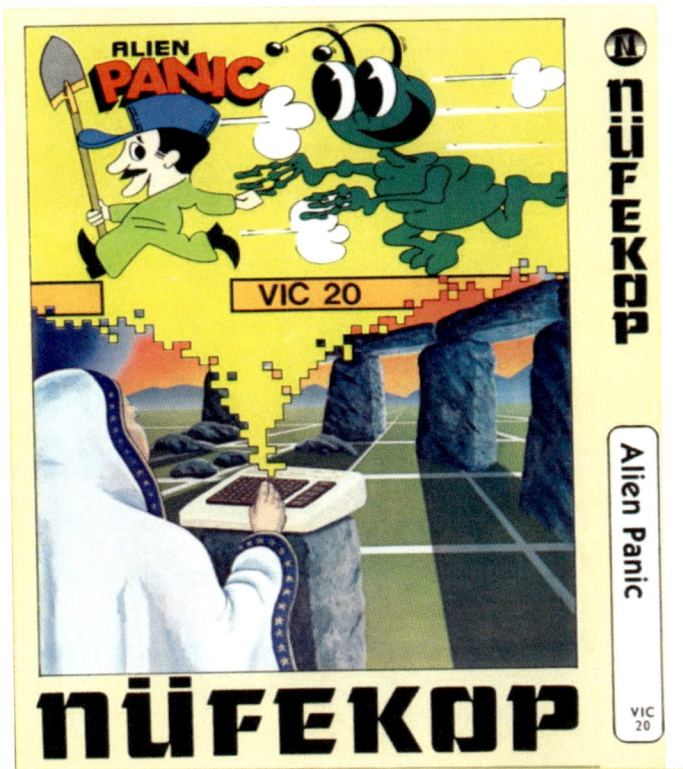

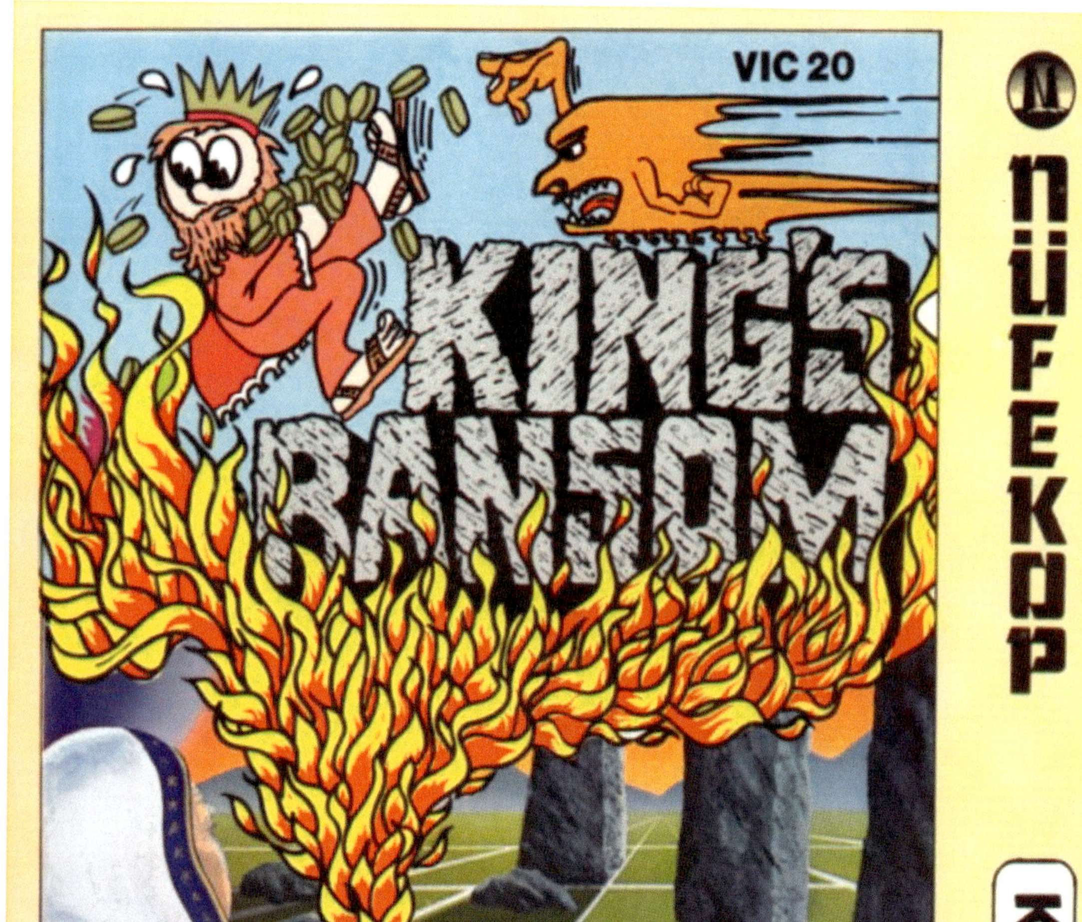
VIC 20
KING'S RANSOM
NÜFEKOP
King's Ransom
VIC 20
NÜFEKOP

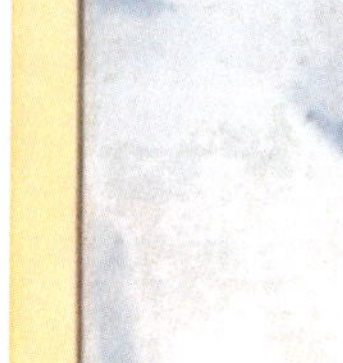

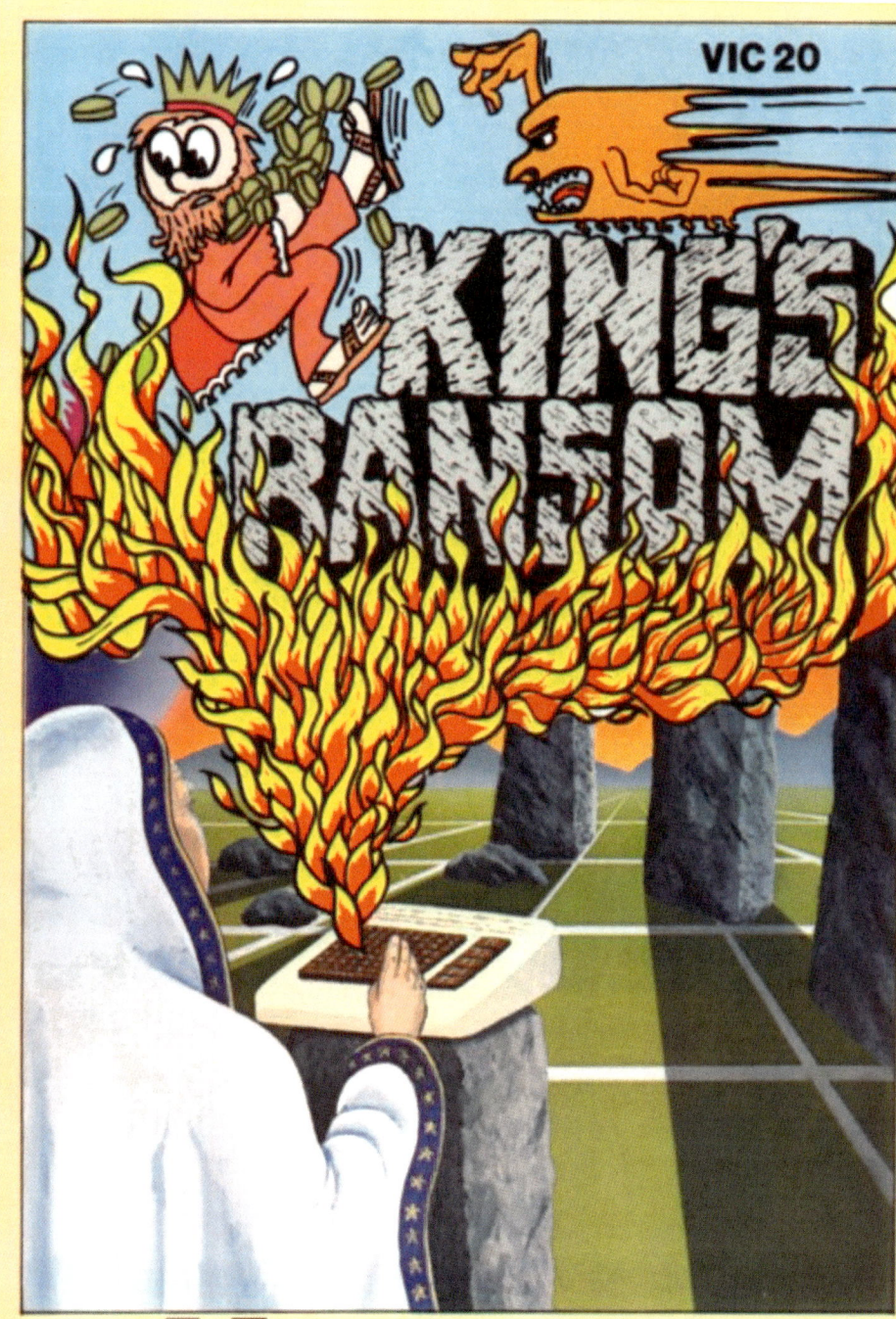

King's Ransom . . .

REQUIRES: Unexpanded VIC20 Home Computer
If Tape version; Commodore Tape Player
If disk version; 1540 or 1541 Disk Drive
Joystick is optional (but suggested)

A demon's foul curse has condemned a king who thought himself capable of striking a bargain with immortals to an eternal half-existance in the five layers of the undead. As a seemingly cruel joke the same demon offered a way of escape. The very gold coins the king had people put to death to possess now hold the only means of return. Your charge is to help the reformed king collect these coins by jumping from moving level to moving level, carefully leaping over all obstacles encountered. This package includes a nice short story entitled "The Thirteenth King".

Contents

☐ Cassette   ☐ Disk   ☐ Cartridge
CG016

More Nufekop Products for the Vic 20!

Exterminator   Racefun
Antimatter Splatter   The Catch
Defender on Tri   Space Quest
Alien Panic   Kings Ransom
Krazy Kong   Music Writer III

nüfekop

VIC 20

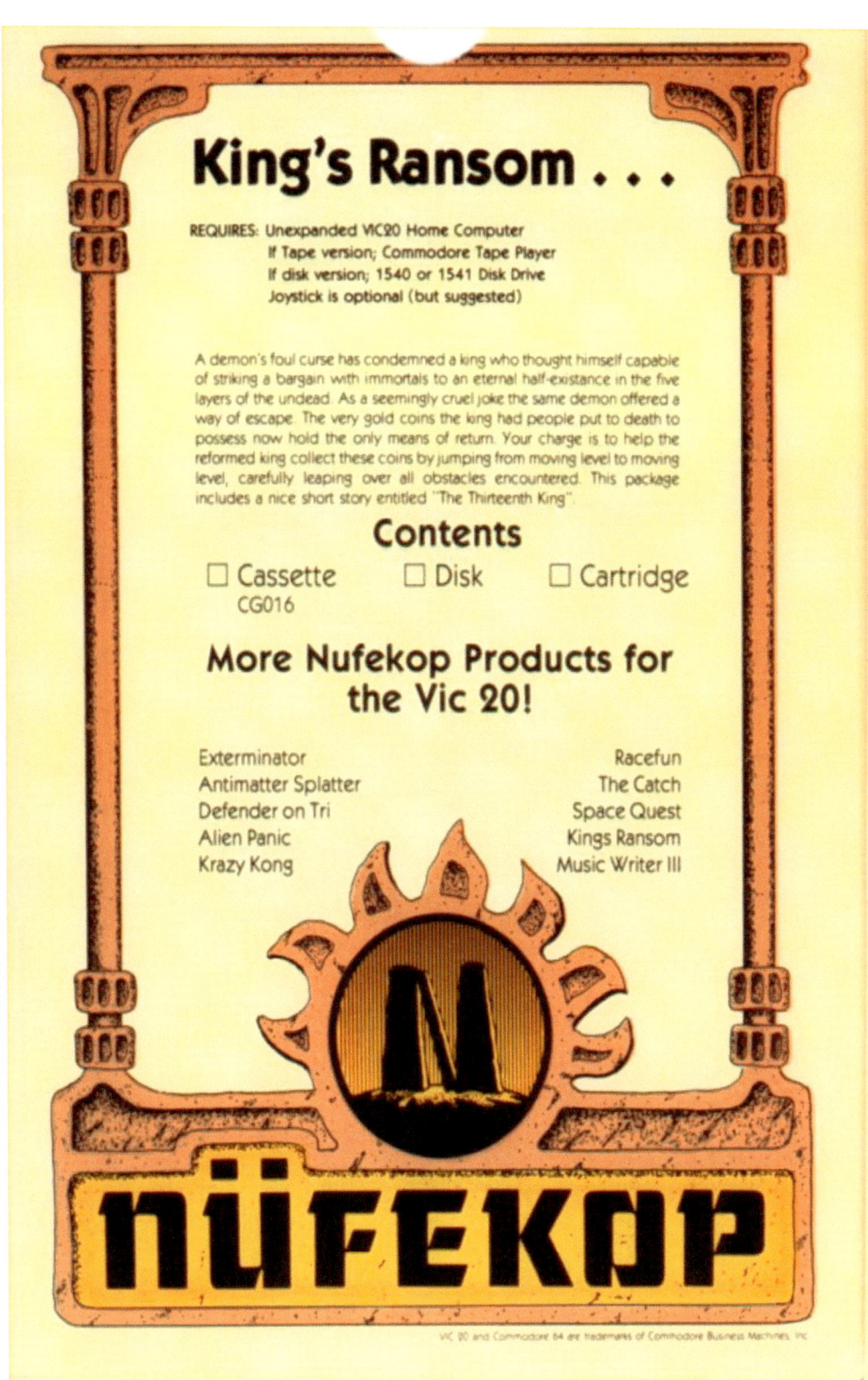

21255 Hwy. 62
P.O. Box 156,
Shady Cove,
Oregon 97539

VIC 20 and Commodore 64 are trademarks of Commodore Business Machines, Inc.

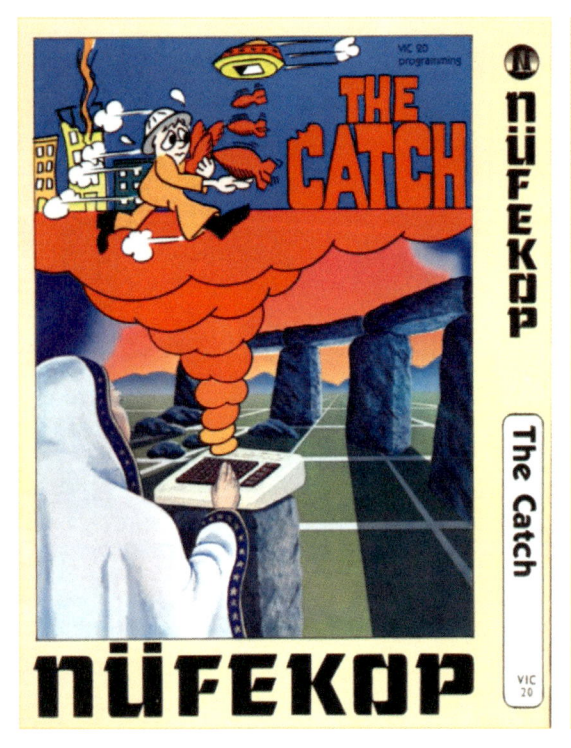

Notice these have a spot to indicate if the contents were cassette, Disk, or Cartridge. We were ready for cartridges but never made the transition.

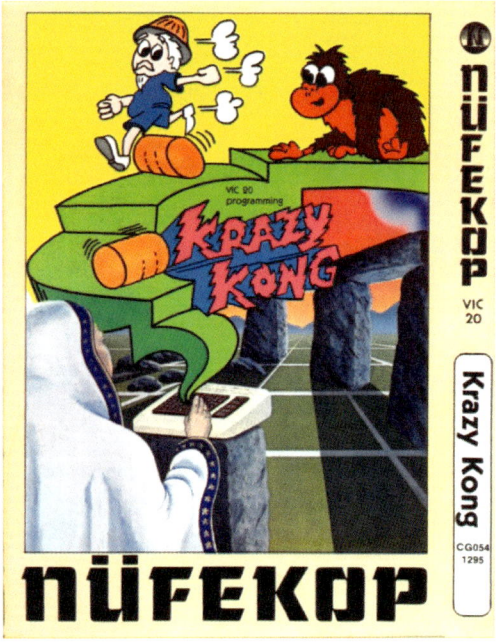

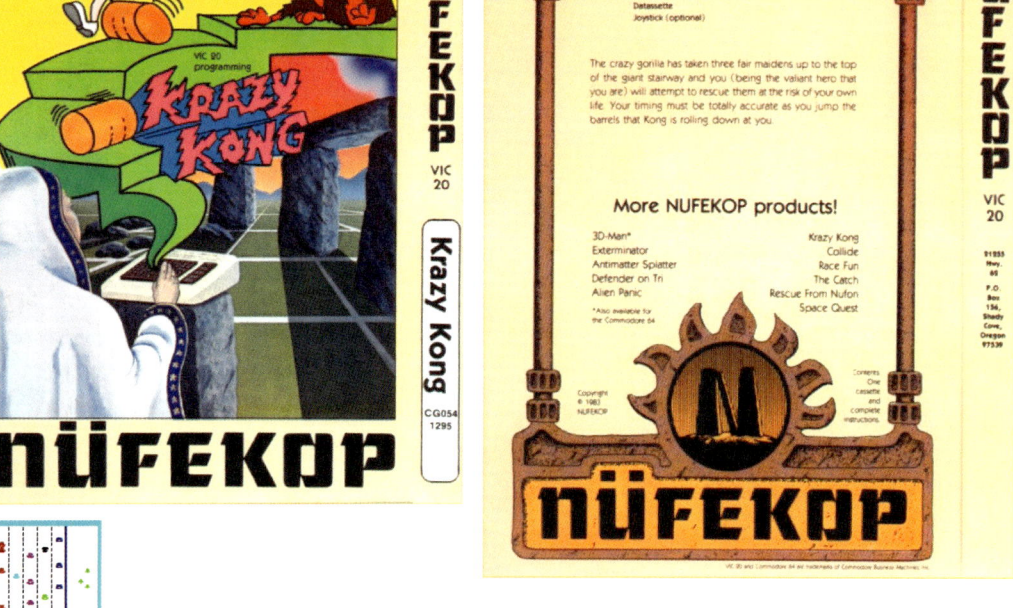

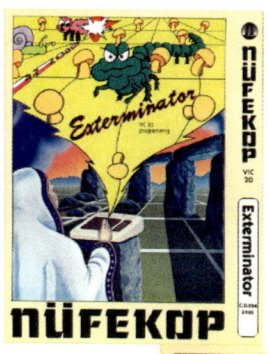

These even shipped with a warranty card. We kept everyone who returned one on file. About 3% mailed them back in.

DEFENDER ON TRI
VIC 20
programming
SKYES LIMITED
NÜFEKOP
Defender on Tri
VIC 20
NÜFEKOP

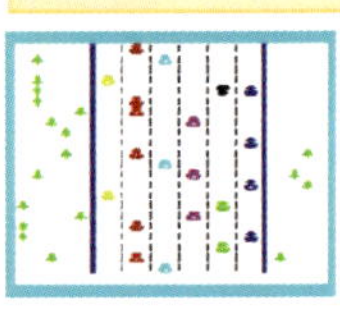

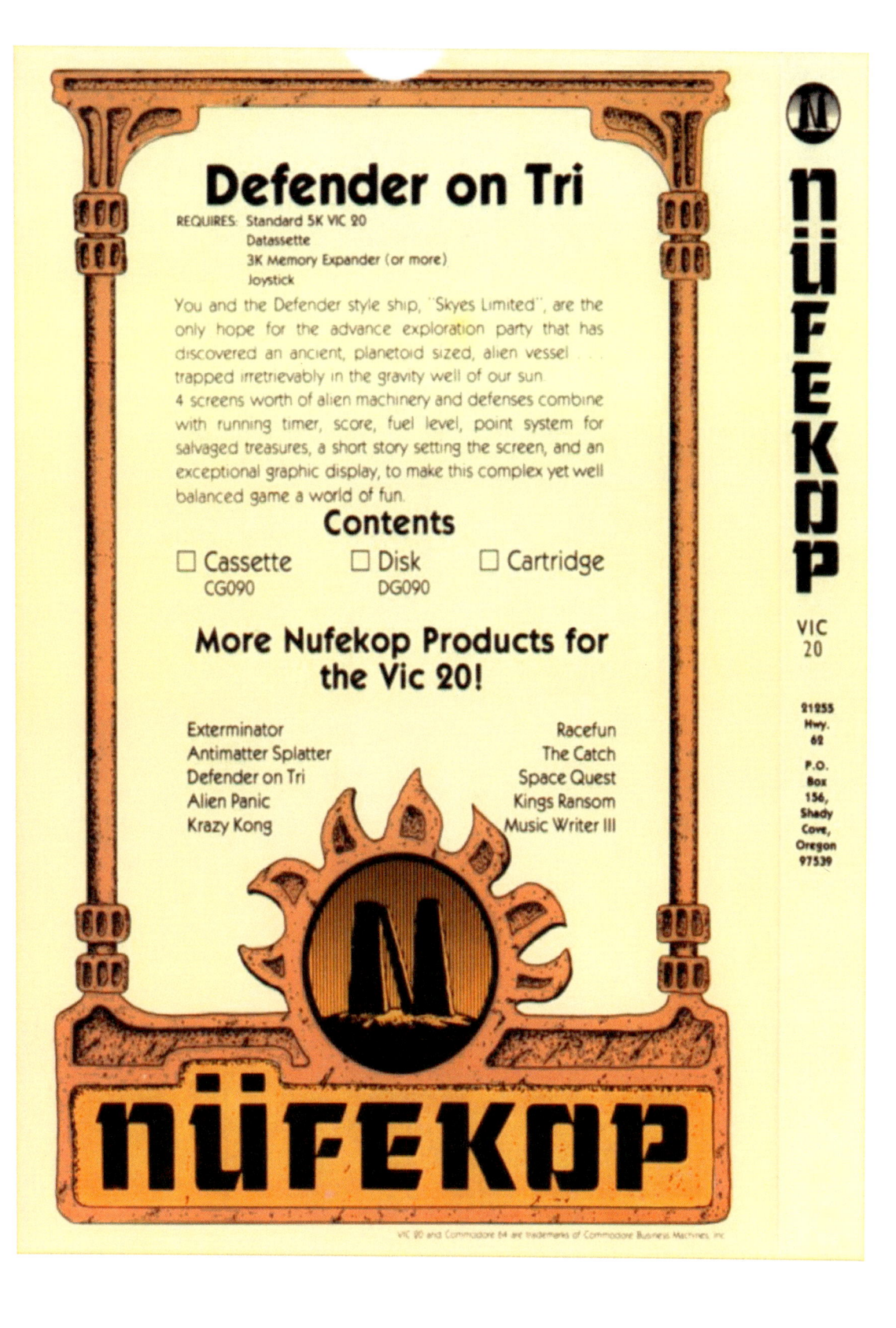

Defender on Tri

REQUIRES: Standard 5K VIC 20
Datassette
3K Memory Expander (or more)
Joystick

You and the Defender style ship, "Skyes Limited", are the only hope for the advance exploration party that has discovered an ancient, planetoid sized, alien vessel... trapped irretrievably in the gravity well of our sun.

4 screens worth of alien machinery and defenses combine with running timer, score, fuel level, point system for salvaged treasures, a short story setting the screen, and an exceptional graphic display, to make this complex yet well balanced game a world of fun.

Contents

☐ Cassette ☐ Disk ☐ Cartridge
CG090   DG090

More Nufekop Products for the Vic 20!

Exterminator
Antimatter Splatter
Defender on Tri
Alien Panic
Krazy Kong

Racefun
The Catch
Space Quest
Kings Ransom
Music Writer III

nüfekop

nüfekop
VIC 20

21255 Hwy. 62
P.O. Box 156,
Shady Cove,
Oregon
97539

VIC 20 and Commodore 64 are trademarks of Commodore Business Machines, Inc.

The Games.

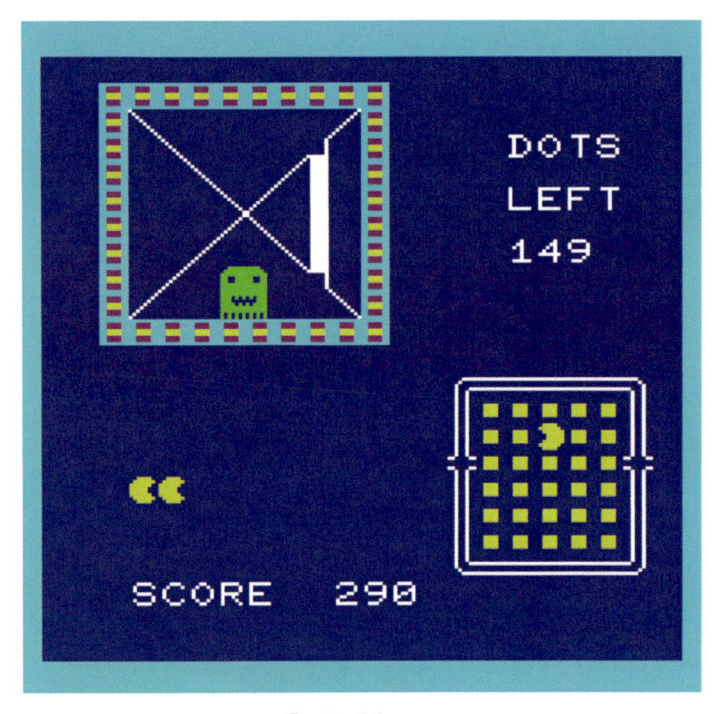

3-D Man was not a very good game, but was a great concept. Every company was looking for a way to do some knock-off of pac man, putting it in a 3-D maze made it a whole different game and got people thinking differently about game design.

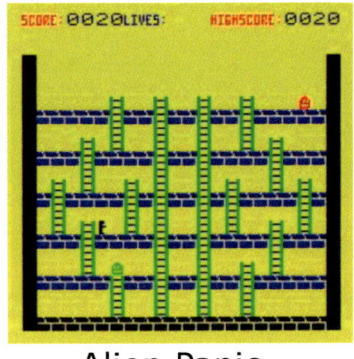

3-D Man

Alien Panic 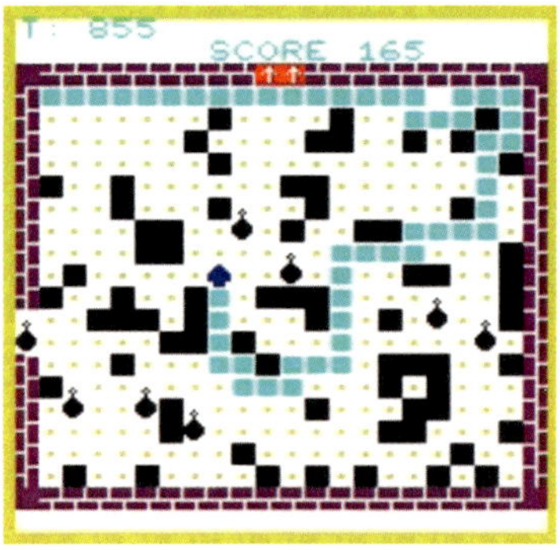   Blowup    Bomber

Collide 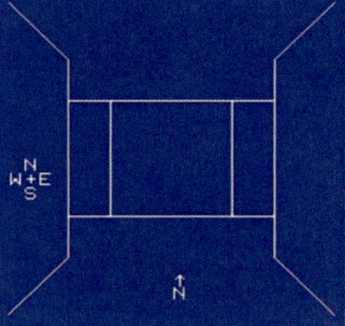   Escape 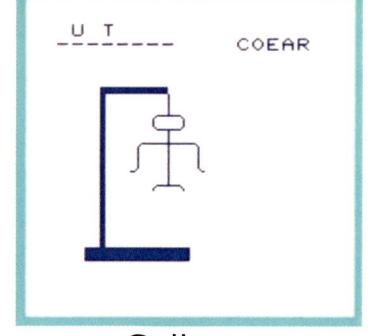   Gallows

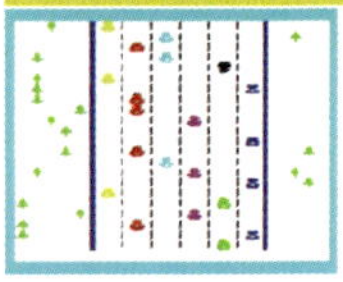

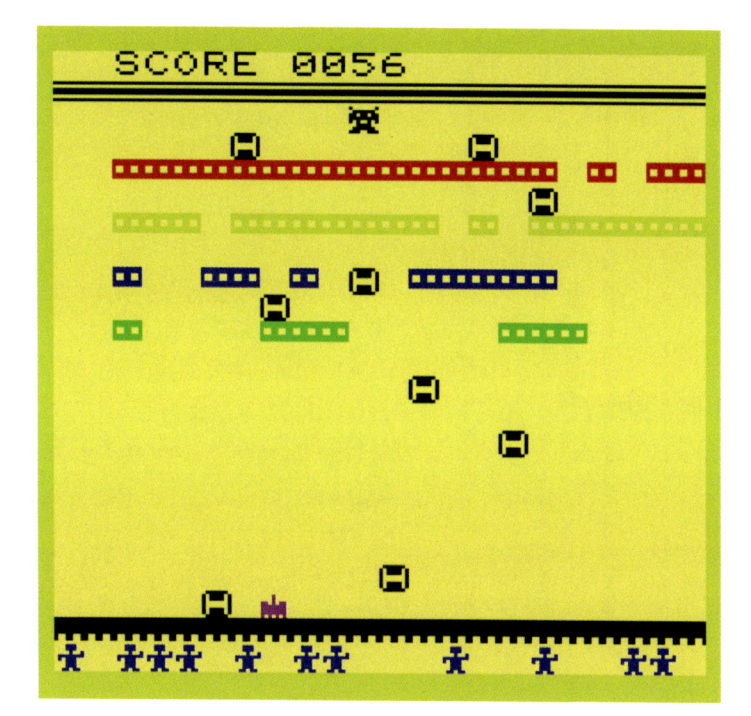

Anti-Matter Splatter not only had a fun name, but was my first 100% machine code game. The goal was to have the entire screen in motion, just because I could! It also made extensive use of swapping character definitions so it had smooth graphics.

Anti-Matter Splatter

Defender on Tri required a 3k or 8k memory expansion. It was our first game to do that. Documentation about the expanders was sparse, so a lot of trial and error went into figuring out how to support the various configurations of ram. The ship, "Skyes Limited" was named after Gary's son Skye.

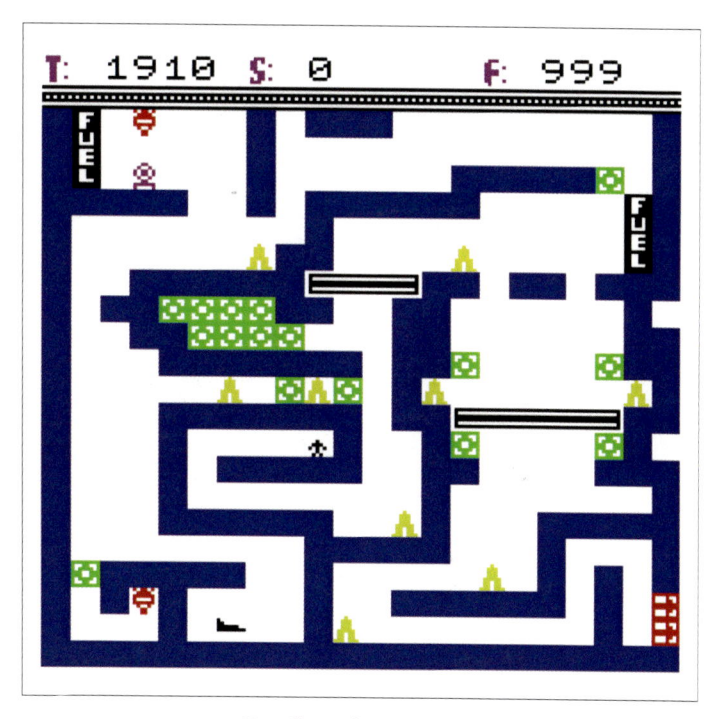

Defender on Tri

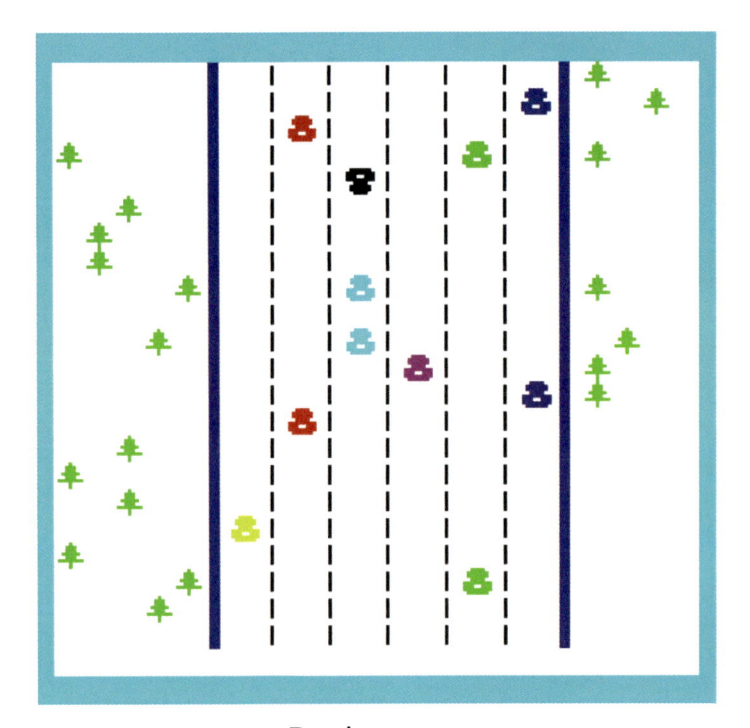

Dodgecars was one of our very first games, but was also destined to be one of our favorites and most played. It's frustrating, but you always feel like you can score a little better on it. All you have to do is dodge the other cars!
My current high score is 539!

Dodgecars

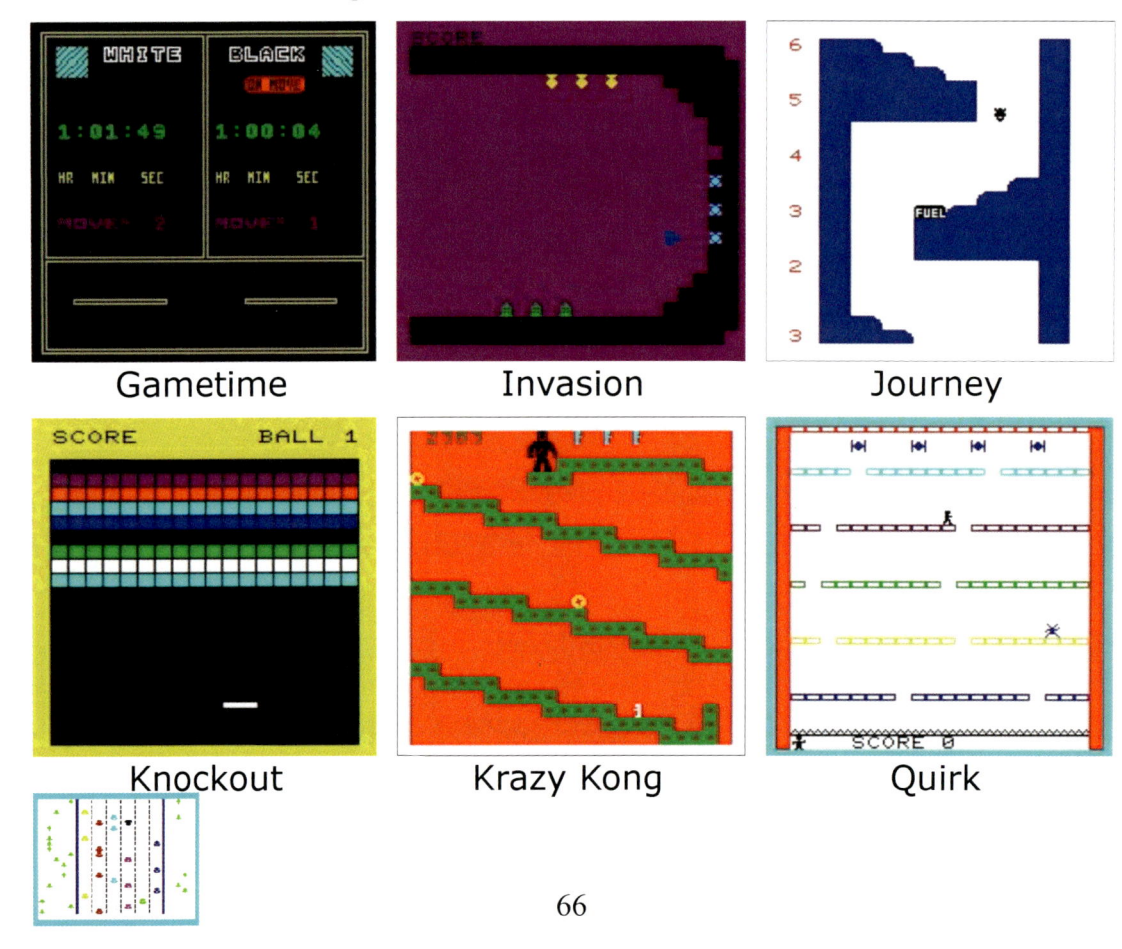

Gametime

Invasion

Journey

Knockout

Krazy Kong

Quirk

Kings Ransom was one of our last Vic 20 games and was one of the best. It used a mini array of bits to represent the screen layouts so it had lots of levels, lots of enemies, and the player could run and jump all over the screen. Very fun!

Kings Ransom

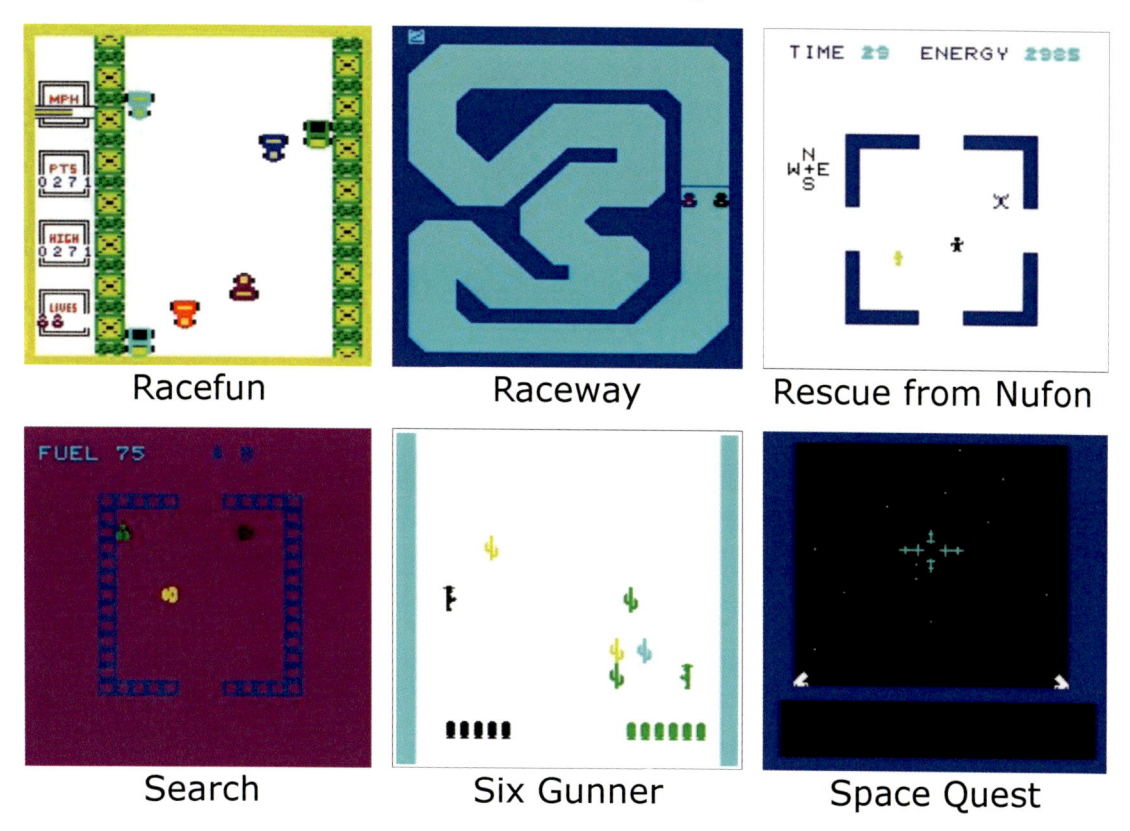

Racefun

Raceway

Rescue from Nufon

Search

Six Gunner

Space Quest

The Catch was simple, but super fun. All machine language, it was super fast and weeded out amateur players in a few seconds.
It was an instant hit and ran on a standard 3k Vic.

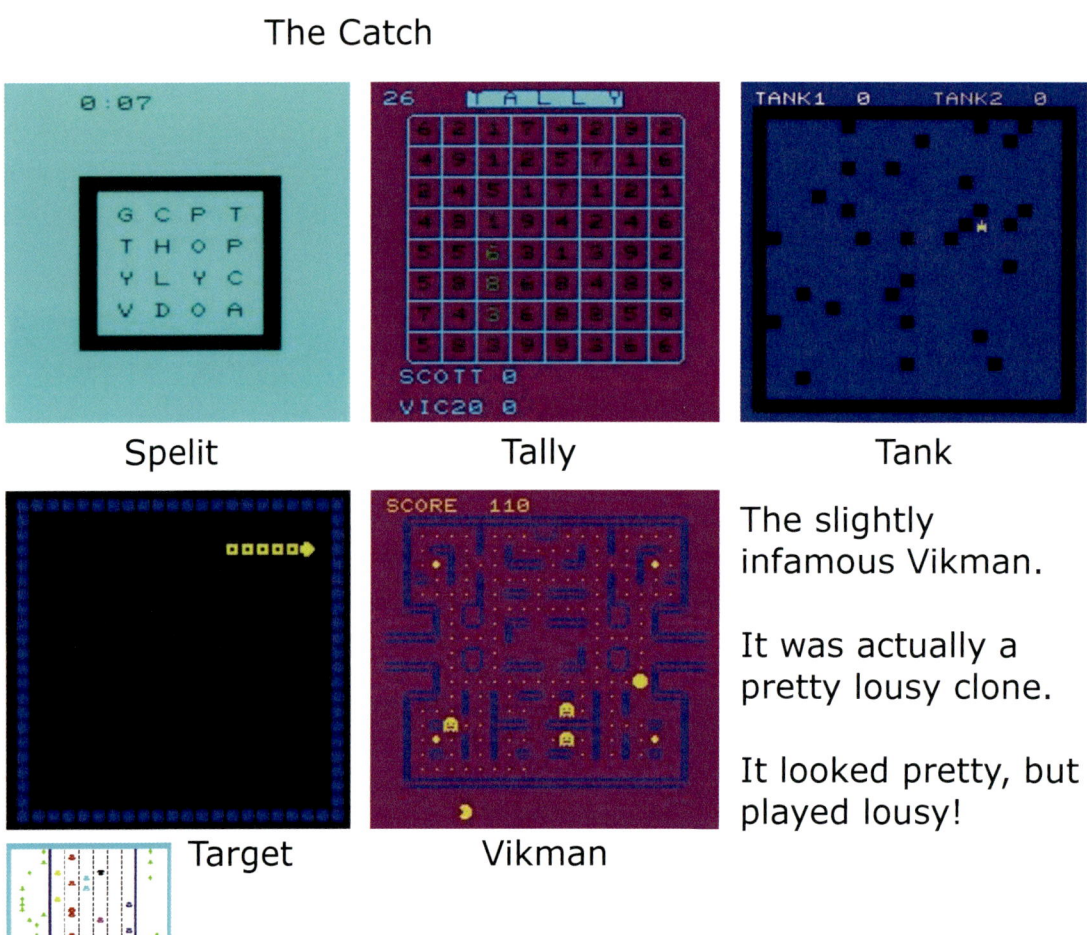

The Catch

Spelit

Tally

Tank

Target

Vikman

The slightly infamous Vikman.

It was actually a pretty lousy clone.

It looked pretty, but played lousy!

68

Prototypes.
Several games didn't make it to production for various reasons. Some were too buggy, some too simple, some just not fun.

Chaos
This game design never got on it's feet. I think you were chasing stuff and the maze continuously changed out from under you.

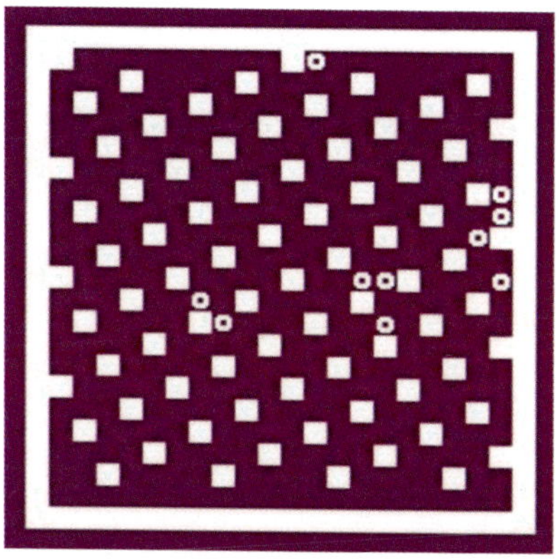

Football
This was similar to those handheld football games. Was nearly finished and fun, but could never dial in the difficulty as you progressed.

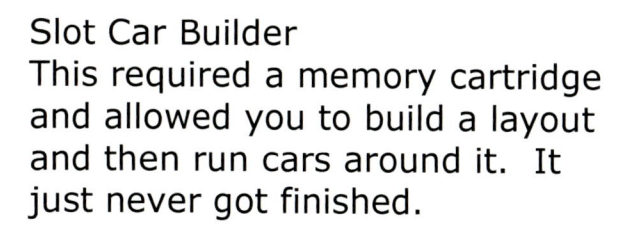

Slot Car Builder
This required a memory cartridge and allowed you to build a layout and then run cars around it. It just never got finished.

Invaders 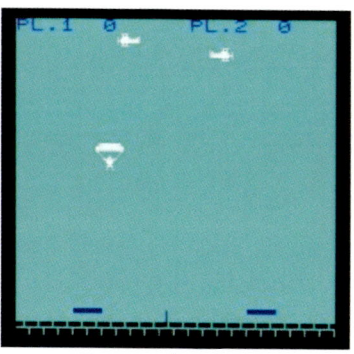   Parachuter 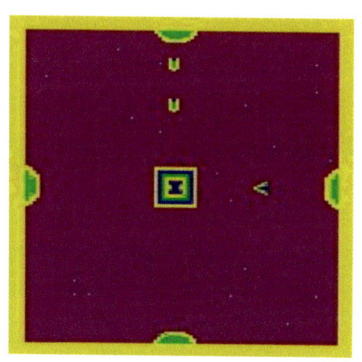   Space Base

Republished.

A lot of Nüfekop games were published outside the U.S. by various companies. The most famous was Bubble Bus, a huge reseller in the U.K. Here's some pictures of the products from the licensees.

70

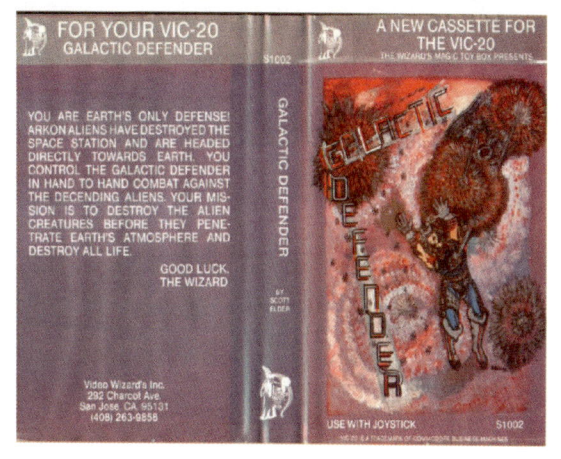

Pirates.

Some Nüfekop software was blatantly pirated, here's some examples. They were lazy pirates, they even left my name on the start up screens and in the code!

Other Products.

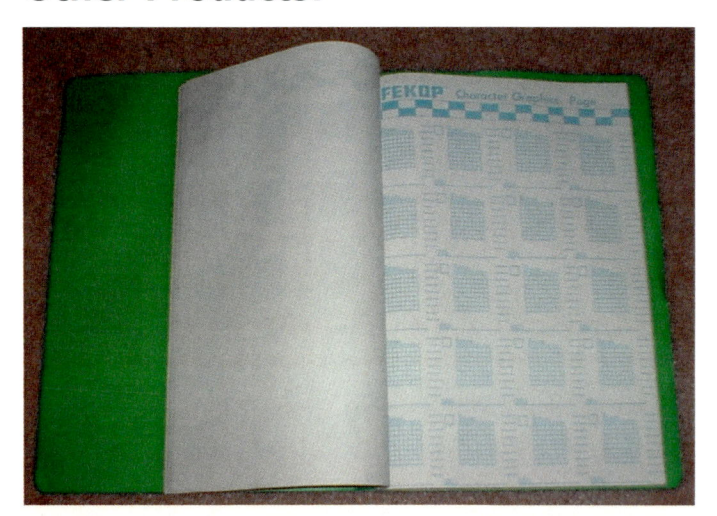

We sold a few other products.

Some were tools to help programmers, like pre-printed sheets to develop screen and character sets.

We also had the famous Meteor and Bird cover for your Commodore computer.

It read: *Wait! Don't stop reading just because you are one of those action types who went out and spent a bundle on one of those cumbersome and hard-to-maintain force field type protectors immediately after acquiring your vic.*

Our meteor and bird covers come with a nice picture of a VIC 20 silk-screened on the top and are available in three colors: blue, beige and brown (please specify B, B or B).

Get this, I just heard that some non-creative types are using them for (this is rich) DUST COVERS!

Well I guess it takes all kinds.

These are a couple prototypes that had a solid rubber surface that would have been quite waterproof. Crazy colors.

73

Developer Support.

Here are some developer documents, a royalty sheet and non-disclosure agreement.

There were also software tools to help developers create artwork.

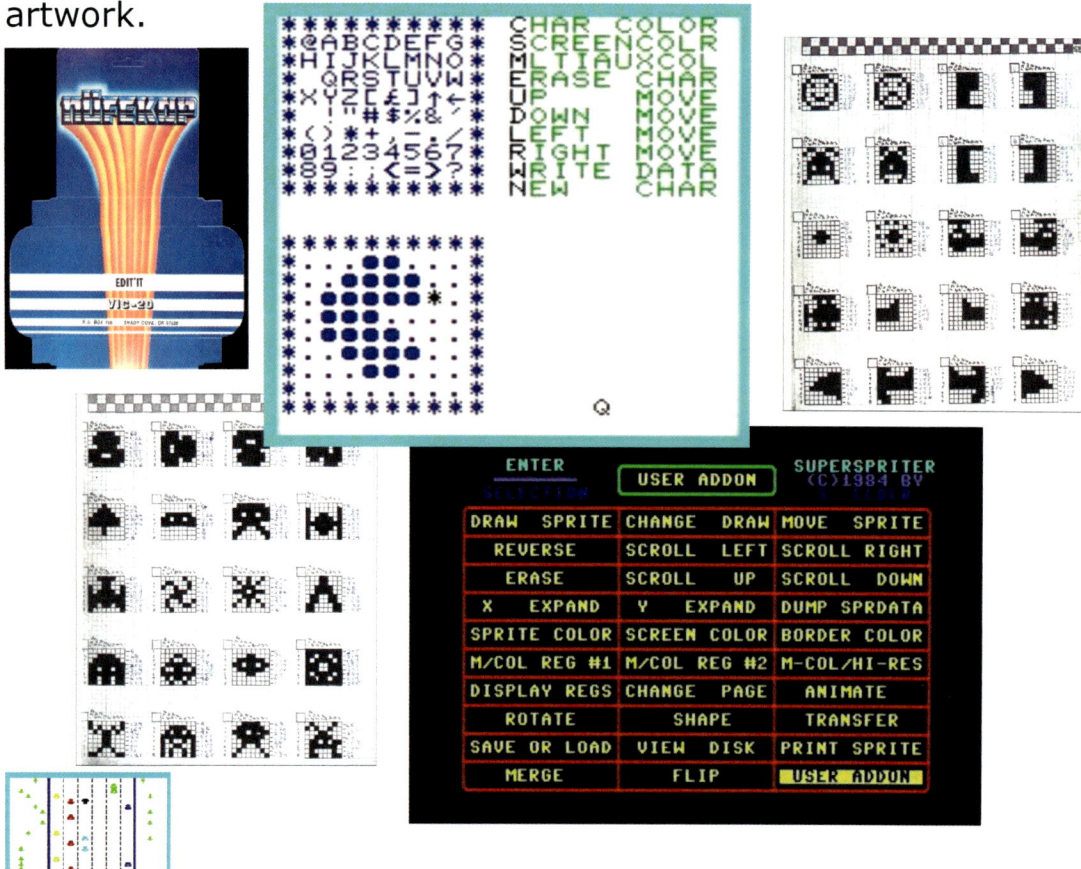

74

Press.
Being one of the first Vic 20 publishers, we got a fair amount of press, which back then consisted mostly of magazine articles.

And some local news stories as well.

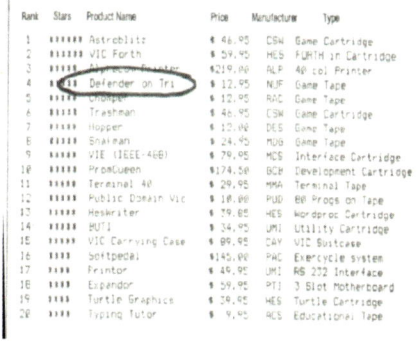

75

Second Catalog.
By the second catalog, a lot had happened. We had a much cleaner look throughout the book.

Here is a "review" of the new games from the desk of the Nüfekop janitor. I'm pretty sure Gary wrote it, but I'm not sure I ever saw him clean up the office!

nüFEKOP

★ From the Desk of the Nufekop Janitor ★
A Solicited Testimonial

As holder of one of the most prestigious positions in the Nufekop structure and in light of my unique familiarity with all their games past and present (I work by myself on night shift and have pass keys to just about everything! — and maybe they're right, I just might owe them a favor) they have insisted that I share my knowledge and expert opinions on the games and goings on around here.

These last four! Whew! You can't imagine how many times (since I found the disk with these games on it) I have been forced to hurry through, or been unable to complete, the tasks I temporarily find myself obliged by contract to perform. With all the money I figure these guys are bringing in, I can't even see why they get so upset at just a little dirt and maybe a few scattered papers, but I'm learning machine language, and when I start selling my games.... All right, already, I'll get back to what I was writing about, you don't have to threaten me, jeez!

O.K. Looking over these four new ones, some impressions develop. Let me share them with you.

(1) A much more in-depth approach to the technical problems (and solutions) that occur during construction of a game. Let me point out for examples the complexities of 3-D Man's maze and radar, the graphics of Defender on TRI, the fact that nearly the entire screen is moving on Anti-Matter Splatter, and the sounds and feel of the stick on Exterminator!

(2) A maturing process seems to have taken place and a new very polished approach to game theory has become evident. This important segment of the making of a well-rounded game is too often overlooked. In simplification, one might say that they realize that a game has to be based on a concept that is fun.

(3) The distinct possibility I can quit asking for my pay in quarters for the arca... hey, you guys, do I have to keep doing this, come on, I'll do better tonight... I mean it, come on...

nüFEKOP

★ From the Desk of the Nufekop Janitor ★
A Solicited Testimonial

As holder of one of the most prestigious positions in the Nufekop structure and in light of my unique familiarity with all their games past and present (I work by myself on night shift and have pass keys to just about everything!) — and maybe they're right, I just might owe them a favor) they have insisted that I share my knowledge and expert opinions on the games and goings on around here.

These last four! Whew! You can't imagine how many times (since I found the disk with these games on it) I have been forced to hurry through, or been unable to complete, the tasks I temporarily find myself obliged by contract to perform. With all the money I figure these guys are bringing in, I can't even see why they get so upset at just a little dirt and maybe a few scattered papers, but I'm learning machine language, and when I start selling my games.... All right, already, I'll get back to what I was writing about, you don't have to threaten me, jeez!

O.K. Looking over these four new ones, some impressions develop. Let me share them with you.

(1) A much more in-depth approach to the technical problems (and solutions) that occur during construction of a game. Let me point out for examples the complexities of 3-D Man's maze and radar, the graphics of Defender on TRI, the fact that nearly the entire screen is moving on Anti-Matter Splatter, and the sounds and feel of the stick on Exterminator!

(2) A maturing process seems to have taken place and a new very polished approach to game theory has become evident. This important segment of the making of a well-rounded game is too often overlooked. In simplification, one might say that they realize that a game has to be based on a concept that is fun.

(3) The distinct possibility I can quit asking for my pay in quarters from the arca... hey, you guys, do I have to keep doing this, come on, I'll do better tonight... I mean it, come on...

INVASION
Standard 5K VIC 20 — Joystick

Simply a lot of fun describes this one. At the right side of a large cavern are four energy pods. Computer-controlled ships fly through from the left to steal them. You have rockets at the bottom and bombs at the top of the cave at your disposal, but perfect timing is essential.

CG036 .... $9.95

JOURNEY
Standard 5K VIC 20 — Joystick

On a journey into a deep cavern, the depths of which have never been explored, you must dodge rock formations and pick up fuel as you go.

CE106 .... $9.95

KRAZY KONG
Standard 5K VIC 20 — Combination (stick and key)

The crazy gorilla has taken three fair maidens up to the top of the giant stairway and you (the valiant hero) will attempt to rescue them at the risk of your own life. Your timing must be totally accurate as you jump the barrels that Kong is rolling down at you.

CG054 .... $9.95

TIMES +
Standard 5K VIC 20 — Keyboard

How long can it take to find three connecting numbers on a large grid, two of which multiplied, the third added or subtracted from from the product of the first two equal the number VIC has chosen? That's what you will find out in this one. Play against VIC (4 levels) or against another player in this fun and *educational* game.

CG $9.95

It included more programming tips, helping people write their own programs. We never gave it much thought, just seemed like the right thing to do since we were excited about programming. It seems like everyone was back then.

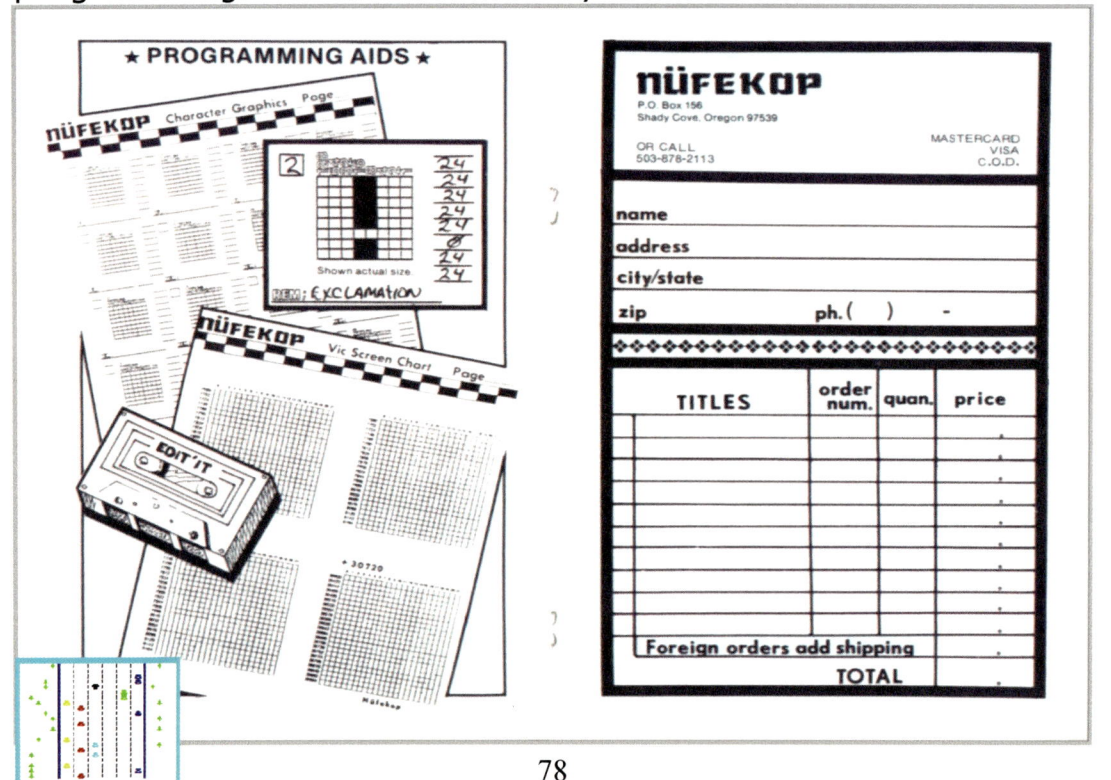

78

Here is the "Big Deal" coupon. Buy 4 get 1 free. Buy 6 get 2 free. A lot of people took us up on this. Gaming was oh so popular in the 80's.

nüFEKOP

A nüfekop *BIG DEAL coupon*

5th game free! with order of 4 or any purchase in excess of $45

or

2 free! with 6 tape order or $65 and up purchase

or

10% discount on under $45 order (subtract from total)

sorry but EXTERMINATOR cannot be chosen as a free game

nüFEKOP

GALLOWS
Standard 5K VIC 20 — Keyboard

Our version of the classic Hangman game plays with over 370 of our words on side one and has skeleton program called "Empty Gallows" on side two for you to enter your own word list. Comes with well-documented, simple, instructions.

CE102 .... $9.95

SPELIT
Standard 5K VIC 20 — Keyboard

This game's strength is that almost uniquely it is playable by the whole family and probably most of their friends at the same time. Though like the letter cube game "Boggle," it does a little more. For instance, a graphic hand shakes the cubes, automatic timer buzzes you when out of time, and provides score-keeping for up to 20 players.

CE106 .... $9.95

SEARCH
Standard 5K VIC 20 — Joystick

Drive a car around a giant maze of rooms picking up moneybags, avoiding a rather aggressive oil slick, and remembering where you were when you last spotted a fuel pump. This very challenging game gives you the feeling you should be able to win it the next time you play it.

CG056 .... $9.95

ALIEN PANIC
Standard 5K VIC 20 — Combination (stick and key)

This arcade-type game pits you against time and an alien on a 6-level construction site with ladders and pitfalls, but not to worry! You have a shovel.

CG008 .... $9.95

nüFEKOP

VIKMAN
Standard 5K VIC 20 — Combination (stick and key)

Another arcade-type game, the problem here is how to eat all the dots and power dots in the maze without being eaten by the 1 to 3 monsters (your choice) that inhabit it.

CG002 .... $9.95

BOMBER
Standard 5K VIC 20 — Combination (stick and key)

Being in charge of three different aircrafts on a mission to clear out a canyon is never easy. You must pick your target carefully and drop your bombs quickly and accurately to avoid wasting precious time. Easy to catch on to, but hard to master.

CG014 .... $9.95

Something for the USERS

EDIT'IT

After some phone calls asking for a good character editor we decided "Hey, we'll sell ours." That seemed simple enough. After one month of trying to make it "user friendly," we were literally covered with bug bites, but had in our possession a polished, finely tuned program. One interesting feature worth the price of admission is the multicolored character mode. Some other features are instant clearing of old character if desired, ability to move character up, down, left, right inside grid. A very useful program.

nüFEKOP

CHARACTER GRAPHIC & SCREEN CHARTS

These started out being made up for personal use but are so convenient we went to the printer and said make a bunch. He did, we put them in notebooks (3-hole binder type), and they are now yours for the ordering.

CASSETTE TAPES

These high-quality data tapes are a must for you buccaneers our there, and are handy for the rest of us. Minimum order of 5. Call for prices on orders of over 50. Our C10 (5 minutes per side) tapes come with hard Norelco boxes.

CG 201	Edit'It	$12.95
NA 202	Character Graphics	4.50
NA 203	Screen Charts	4.50
CO 205	Package of all the above	17.95
NA 204	C10 blank cassettes.............	1.00 each

FINALLY AVAILABLE!
METEOR SHOWER PROTECTION FOR YOUR VIC!

WAIT! Don't stop reading just because you are one of those action types who went out and spent a bundle on one of those cumbersome and hard-to-maintain force field-type protectors immediately after acquiring your VIC. Have you ever thought of what might happen if, for instance, a flock of birds were passing through your computer room and unknowingly you trap them inside the perimeters as you wearily retire for the night? I'll bet not. It's not a pretty sight to wake up to.

Our meteor and bird covers come with a nice picture of the VIC 20 silkscreened on them and are available in three colors: blue, beige and brown (please specify B, B or B).

Get this! I just heard that some non-creative types are using them for (this is rich) **DUST COVERS!** Well, I guess it takes all kinds.

Meteor and bird covers . $6.99

79

There were also a lot of flyers going out at this time.

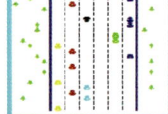

More Nufekop Products for the Vic 20!

FUN AND FULFILLING!

STANDARD UNEXPANDED VIC 20

ALIEN PANIC
By Scott Elder

Climb ladders, bury aliens, and race against time in an abandoned construction site. Joystick.

ANTIMATTER SPLATTER
By Scott Elder

Using your splatter cannon, first to knock holes in the force fields, then to save the population from antimatter canisters that fall faster and faster. Joystick optional.

EXTERMINATOR
By Ken Grant

It is a real challenge to debug this program. It's also a lot of fun. Scorpions, spiders, and centepedes are among the ones you'll run into against the mushroom patch background. Joystick or Trac ball optional.

KRAZY KONG
By Scott Elder

One of our earliest. You are the girl at the top of the stairs only hope but there is this gorilla rolling barrels... Younger people really like this one. Joystick optional.

RACEFUN
By Scott Elder

Fast, flashy, and frustrating. The frustrating part comes when you get caught up in trying to set a new high score and miss business appointments, dinner, and sleep. Joystick optional.

the catch...
By Scott Elder

We've all pondered the age old question about whether one catch shield operated by one person can catch everything one alien can throw at one's city. Till now one could only speculate. Don't forget The Catch. Joystick optional.

KINGS RANSOM
By Scott Elder

Restore a young king's honour by gathering all the tumbling gold coins he sold his soul for earlier. Trapped in the five levels of the undead with spirits of those he put to death to get the very coins that now offer his only hope, he must jump floor to floor, over, and around these spirits with great dexterity and skill or all is lost. You must see and play this game to believe it. Comes with a nice short story booklet entitled 'The Thirteenth King'. Joystick.

EXPANDED MEMORY VIC 20

DEFENDER ON TRI
By Scott Elder

Pilot a small rescue ship through four screens worth of alien machinery. Dormant for a millenium, it has suddenly come to life (probably heat from the sun, it is locked irretrievably on collision course) trapping advance party of scientists. Requires at least 3k memory expander and joystick.

3-D MAN
By Scott Elder

The maze from probably the most popular arcade game ever, with perspective changed from overhead to eye level. It actually has become a kind of 'explore the hallways and eat the dots' adventure game with the ghosts visits to keep you on your toes. Requires at least 3k memory expansion and joystick.

SPACE QUEST
By Scott Elder

Jump your way around the galaxy in your state of the art subspace ship 'Skye's Limited II'. Using the galaxy map to find the enemy machines and to plot your jumps is simple, but when they mess up your jump coordinates and you come out in an asteroid belt flying by the seat of your pants or when you need fuel and must negotiate cave to center of asteroid for hidden deposit, it's not. Requires at least 8k memory expansion. Uses both keyboard and joystick.

Music Writer III
By David Funte

Finding the existing music composing programs slow, complicated, and lacking in storage capacity, author Dave Funte undertook to change the situation, and he has. Minimum number of questions asked per note, very tight machine code, and 500 note capacity is how. Saves and loads your compositions. Outstandingly convenient editing features. Keyboard.

SPECIAL OFFER

THE NUFEKOP SIX PAC, Any six Vic 20 Titles for only $29.95 to our mail order customers.

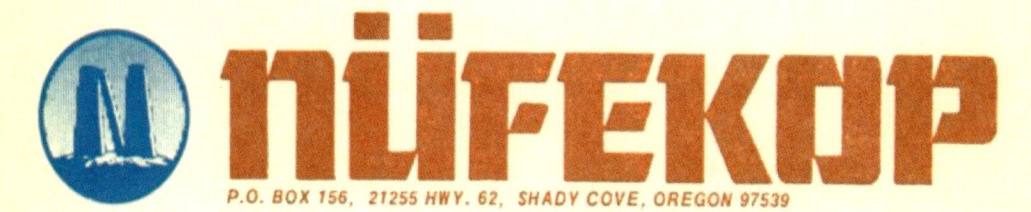

nüfekop

P.O. BOX 156, 21255 HWY. 62, SHADY COVE, OREGON 97539

EXPANDED MEMORY VIC 20 GAMES

(CG090) DEFENDER ON TRI $19.95
PILOT A DEFENDER STYLE SHIP ON MISSION TO SAVE TRAPPED SCIENTISTS FROM A FIERY FATE (they are aboard an alien vessel deep in the gravity well of sol). EXCELLENT GRAPHICS. SHORT SCENE SETTING STORY IN THE INSTRUCTIONS. "DEFENDER ON TRI" REQUIRES AT LEAST 3K ADDED MEMORY.

(CG092) 3D MAN $19.95
THE MAZE FROM PROBABLY THE MOST POPULAR ARCADE GAME EVER, WITH PERSPECTIVE ALTERED FROM OVERHEAD TO EYE LEVEL. THE DOTS, THE MONSTERS, THE POWER DOTS, THE SIDE EXITS, THE GAME IS AMAZING. "3D MAN" REQUIRES AT LEAST 3K ADDED MEMORY.

(CG088) SPACE QUEST $19.95
OUR FIRST 8K MEMORY EXPANDER GAME AND ITS A BEAUTY. THE SCENE (a short story is included) IS FAR IN THE FUTURE, A TIME WHEN MAN'S KNOWLEDGE HAS REDUCED AN ENTIRE GALAXY INTO A MAPPED SERIES OF QUADRANTS. THIS GAME HAS STRATAGY (you plot your own hyperspace jumps on Galaxy map), ACTION (against a starry background you find yourself engaged in a dogfight, laser style), EXPLORATION (you must fly your ship deep into caverns to pick up necessary fuel). "SPACE QUEST" REQUIRES AT LEAST 8K MEMORY EXPANSION AND A JOYSTICK.

COMMODORE 64

(CG602) 3D-64, MAN $19.95
THIS AVAILABLE ON THE EXPANDED "VIC 20" GAME, HAS BEEN COMPLETELY REWRITTEN FOR THE 64 AND USES SPRITES, SOUNDS, AND OTHER FEATURES NOT AVAILABLE ON THE "VIC". THIS ONE REQUIRES A JOYSTICK.

*nüFEKOP

TWO OF THE 4 SCREENS FROM NUFEKOP'S DEFENDER ON TRI.

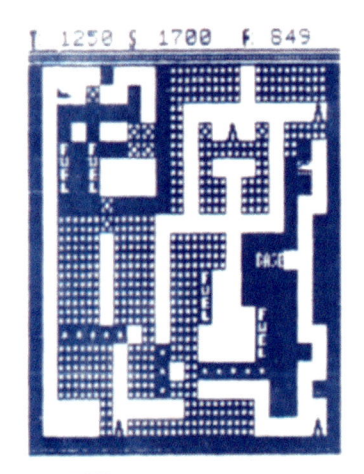

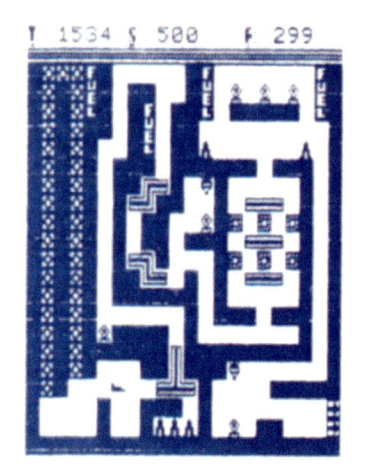

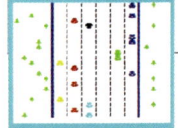

Cassettalogs.

We were the first that I know of to offer a catalog on other media besides paper. Our first was the Cassettalog, a software program on tape that had screen shots of the games, tips and tricks, a free game and more.

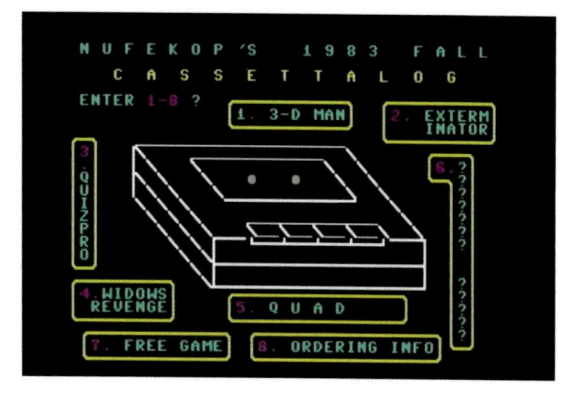

And once diskettes were in use, we quickly sent out a Diskettalog!

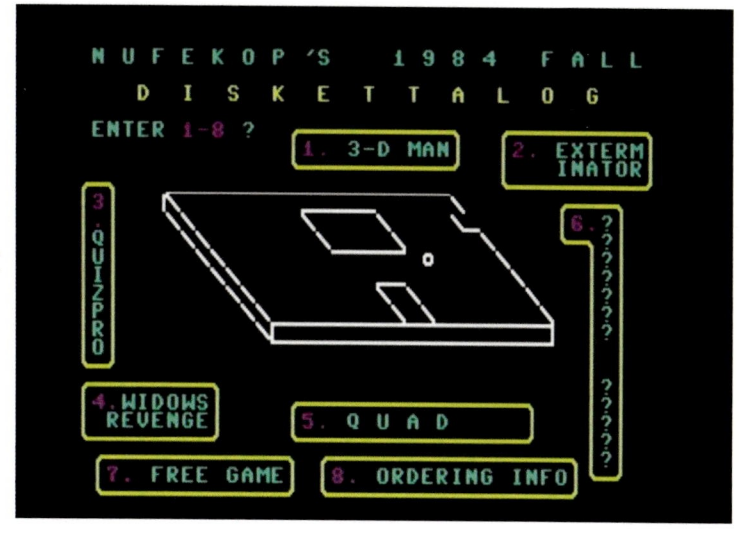

Diskettes.

After thousands and thousands of cassette tapes, the move was on to 5 ¼ inch floppies. The product line was slimmed down at about this same point in time, so most games were available on disk.

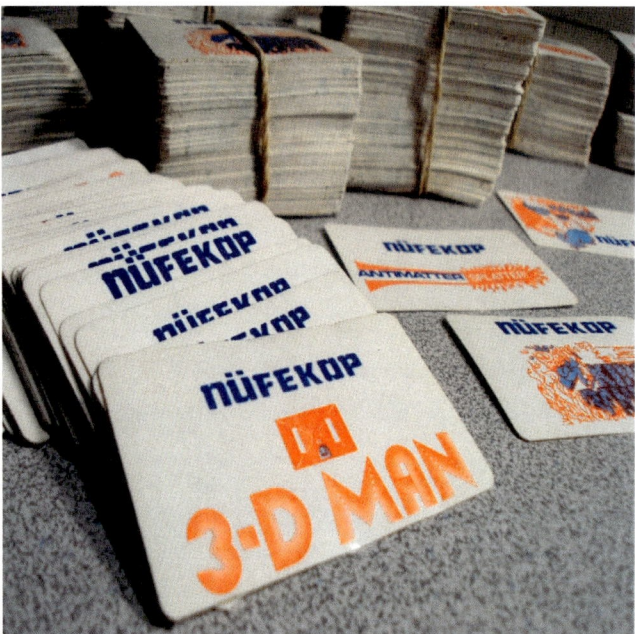

Just like cassettes, once we were shipping discs, we needed a lot of labels.

We opted for a simple sticker that could be used for any purpose.

There was also pressure to release games on cartridges.

Apparently people had grown weary of turning their cassette players on their sides or upside-down to help convince a stubborn program to load (yes that really did help).

We made some prototypes of several of our games, with hand-etched circuit boards and 2732 eproms, but they were never mass-produced.

If you do manage to find one, you've got a pretty rare piece of hardware. There are probably less than 15 in existance.

The 64.
We did several products for the C-64, here's a brief look.

More?
Sure, there's more pictures and stuff to show you, but I think there's enough preserved here to please me... and I hope you've enjoyed it too.

The actual programs themselves are preserved well on the internet. There is a lot of "retro" gaming going on, so there are many websites that have gathered up these old games and offer them as free downloads. If you enjoy these vintage games you should support the sites that have them. Using emulators such as "Winvice" you can have a pretty nice virtual Vic 20 or C-64 on your personal computer.

What happened to Nüfekop?
The game crash that began in 1984 took out most game publishers big and small and Nüfekop was no exception. There were far too many companies trying to gain market share and enthusiasts grew tired of having new games and hardware forced on them every day. Nüfekop went from selling several thousand games a month to a few dozen almost overnight. Similar stories were heard from publishers all over the country.

It was very fun times. Discovery, invention and learning happened daily. I really wanted to share the pictures and stories before they were forgotten. Maybe now the kids will understand their Dad's game obsession just a bit better, knowing I was involved at the start.

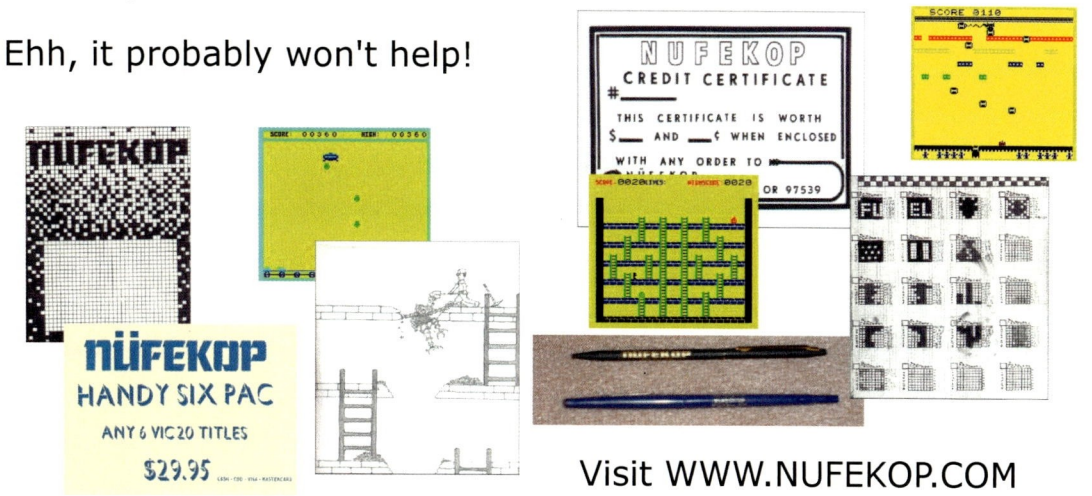

Ehh, it probably won't help!

Visit WWW.NUFEKOP.COM

POKEFUN

GAME COMPANY
UP A CLASSIC
IMANGLES

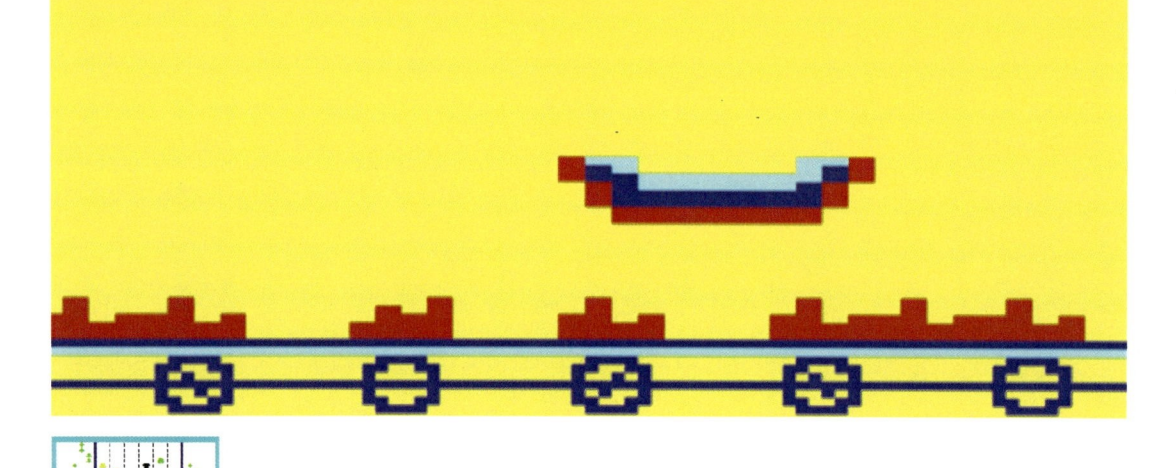

Made in the USA
Las Vegas, NV
05 October 2023